THE COLONIAL MOSAIC

AMERICAN WOMEN
1600-1760

THE YOUNG OXFORD HISTORY OF WOMEN IN THE UNITED STATES

Nancy F. Cott, *General Editor*

THE COLONIAL MOSAIC

AMERICAN WOMEN 1600-1760

Jane Kamensky

OXFORD UNIVERSITY PRESS

New York • Oxford

For Meghan Elizabeth Lodwick

Oxford University Press

Oxford   New York
Athens Auckland Bangkok Bogotá Bombay
Buenos Aires Calcutta Cape Town Dar es Salaam
Delhi Florence Hong Kong Istanbul Karachi
Kuala Lumpur Madras Madrid Melbourne
Mexico City Nairobi Paris Singapore
Taipei Tokyo Toronto Warsaw
and associated companies in
Berlin   Ibadan

Library of Congress Cataloging-in-Publication Data
Kamensky, Jane.
The colonial mosaic : American women 1600–1760 / Jane Kamensky.
p.   cm. — (The young Oxford history of women in the United States ; v. 2)
Includes bibliographical references and index.
ISBN 0-19-508015-7 (library edition); ISBN 0-19-508830-1 (series, library edition)
ISBN 0-19-512400-6 (paperback); ISBN 0-19-512398-0 (series, paperback)
1. Women—United States—History—Juvenile literature.
2. Women—United States—History—18th century—Juvenile literature.
3. United States—History—Colonial period. ca. 1600–1775—Juvenile literature.
[1. Women—History. 2. Women—Social conditions. 3. United States—Social conditions—to 1865.]
I. Title. II. Series.
HQ1410.Y68 1994 vol. 2
[HQ1416]
305.4'0973s—dc20
[305.4'0973'09032]   94-40191
CIP

3 5 7 9 8 6 4 2

Printed in the United States of America on acid-free paper
Design: Leonard Levitsky
Picture research: Patricia Burns, Laura Kreiss

On the cover: Mrs. Freake and Baby Mary, *circa 1671–74,* artist unknown.
Frontispiece: Pocahontas and her son, Thomas Rolfe. This portrait dates from the 18th
century, long after her death in March 1617.

CONTENTS

INTRODUCTION

The United States is known as a nation of immigrants. That theme was first sounded in the 17th century, when groups of settlers from England and Europe began to people the colonies established by Great Britain, Holland, and France on the eastern edges of North America. Confronting and displacing—while also learning from—the Native American inhabitants, these colonists came for many reasons: to practice and institute their religious preferences, to gain land, to make money. Although the story of colonial settlement is often told as if men were the only actors (forming entrepreneurial companies, leading congregations, getting charters from the king), no colony survived without women among its participants. The division of labor between the sexes was not the same among the settlers as it was among the Indians they met, but women as wives, as agricultural workers, as domestic servants, as members of religious congregations, as community builders, and as mothers of a new generation were crucial to the health of European settlements just as women in Native American groups complemented their men in their social organization.

The communities initially established by European settlers in the "New World" varied greatly by region, both because of geography and environment and because different groups of settlers var-

The responsibilities of Hopi women were not limited to child rearing and basket weaving, as pictured in this 20th-century painting by a member of the tribe. Many Native American women also worked in agriculture, built homes, and transported possessions when villages moved.

ied in their aims. All of these settlements, however, changed over the generations, as the first bands of intrepid transatlantic voyagers produced their own children and were joined by ever more diverse groups of immigrants. Their populations would grow and cohere enough by 1776 to unite and call themselves an independent nation. This book tells the stories of women in these changing and growing settlements: diverse women whose forebears came from distant points on the globe, who helped build the complex multicultural society that would call itself the United States.

This book is part of a series that covers the history of women in the United States from the 17th through the 20th century. Traditional historical writing has dealt almost entirely with men's lives because men have, until very recently, been the heads of state, the political officials, judges, ministers, and business leaders who have wielded the most visible and recorded power. But for several recent decades, new interest has arisen in social and cultural history, where common people are the actors who create trends and mark change as well as continuity. An outpouring of research and writing on women's history has been part of this trend to look at individuals and groups who have not held the reins of rule in their own hands but nonetheless participated in making history. The motive to address and correct sexual inequality in society has also vitally influenced women's history, on the thinking that knowledge of the past is essential to creating justice for the future.

The histories in this series look at many aspects of women's lives. The books ask new questions about the course of American history. How did the type and size of families change, and what difference did that make in people's lives? What expectations for women differed from those for men, and how did such expectations change over the centuries? What roles did women play in the economy? What form did women's political participation take when they could not vote? And how did politics change when women did gain full citizenship? How did women work with other women who were like or unlike them, as well as with men, for social and political goals? What sex-specific constraints or opportunities did they face? The series aims to understand the diverse women who have peopled American history by investigating their work and leisure, family patterns, political activities, forms of organization, and outstanding accomplishments. Standard events of American history, from the settling of the continent to the American Revolution, the Civil War, industrialization, American entry onto the world stage, and world wars, are all here, too, but seen from the point of view of women's experiences. Together, the answers to new questions and the treatment of old ones from women's points of view make up a compelling narrative of four centuries of history in the United States.

—Nancy F. Cott

THE YOUNG OXFORD HISTORY OF WOMEN IN THE UNITED STATES

Nancy F. Cott, *General Editor*

King Powhatan comands C: Smith to be slayne,
daughter Pokahontas beggs his life his thankfull.

A MEETING OF MANY WORLDS

Pocahontas, the beloved daughter of one of the most powerful leaders in North America, was little more than a child when strangers from across the Atlantic transformed her world forever. Her people, a group of Algonquian tribes called Powhatans whose lands stretched for miles across parts of what is now the southeastern United States, would have known the Europeans long before Pocahontas herself encountered them. Small bands of traders and adventurers had journeyed from England and Spain to Powhatan territory throughout the 16th century. In 1585, Sir Walter Raleigh, a leader of one of these English companies, had even gone so far as to give their homeland a new name. "Virginia," he had called it, after Elizabeth I, the English ruler known as the Virgin Queen. Thus Pocahontas, born in the mid-1590s, grew up in a world in the midst of momentous changes. For her, those changes came to a head in December 1607. It was then, at the age of 11 or 12, that she first found herself in a position that would become a familiar one for many Native American women. She was caught, in what must have been confusing and even painful circumstances, between two profoundly different cultures.

On one side of this divide was the world of her father, Chief Powhatan, who had united diverse bands of Algonquians into a loose-

In this illustration from Captain John Smith's Generall Historie of Virginia *(1624), Pocahontas pleads with her father, Chief Powhatan, to spare Smith's life.*

Captain John Smith, one of the leaders of the English settlement at Jamestown. One of the first phrases he learned in the Powhatan dialect concerned the young Pocahontas.

knit confederacy in the 1570s. Striving to protect the confederacy from the European invaders who had recently erected a settlement they called Jamestown (named after their king), Powhatan took John Smith, one of the English leaders, prisoner. The English had, in just a few short months, already established a pattern of tense and often violent relations with the Powhatans. Smith stood accused of having murdered two of Pocahontas's people and, by Powhatan custom, faced execution for his crime.

On the other side of a wide cultural rift—but also increasingly a part of Pocahontas's changing world—stood John Smith and his people. By the December evening Powhatan had selected for Smith's execution, Pocahontas had known the English captain for some months. Since the previous June, when Smith's band of settlers first arrived in what they called the "New World" (to Pocahontas, of course, it was a very *old* world indeed), Pocahontas had spent time trading and talking among them. She taught them to communicate in her language, and she learned bits of Smith's language as well. Indeed, she had learned more than merely English *words*. Her time among the settlers at Jamestown had also taught her something about English ways of seeing, about how they understood this "new" world.

We can imagine, therefore, that Pocahontas would have regarded the scene that unfolded in her father's dwelling on that December night in 1607 with a kind of doubled vision. From one angle she would have seen the ceremony in which, as Smith later described it in his *Generall Historie of Virginia*, Powhatan's advisers forced Smith's head onto two "great stones" and prepared to "beate out his braines" with clubs as a just and natural punishment for an awful crime. At the same time, however, she seemed to feel sympathy for her father's prisoner and horror at the violent death he was about to suffer. In this sense, she also saw the scene through English eyes: with fear and repulsion.

That, at least, is what John Smith later claimed. According to his *Generall Historie*, Pocahontas's "civilized" half took over at the very moment he was about to lose his life. She entreated her father to stop the execution. When her words failed, she strode into the center of the assembly and intervened bodily. Bending over the terrified captain, she took Smith's "head in her armes, and laid her owne upon his to save him from death." Struck by his daughter's bravery and devotion, according to Smith, Powhatan experienced a change of heart and declared himself "contented" that the prisoner "should live."

The moment she put her life in jeopardy to save John Smith's, Pocahontas changed the course of American history. Instead of being executed as a brutal murderer, Smith entered into a more harmonious relationship with his former enemies. By saving the life of an important leader during a politically unstable time, Pocahontas likely prevented the struggling settlement at Jamestown from suffering the fate of Roanoke, the "lost" English colony that had van-

Ætatis suæ 21. Aº.1616.

...oaks als Rebecka daughter to the mighty Prince ...hatan Emperour of Attanoughkomouck als Virginia ...erted and baptized in the Christian faith, and ...Wife to the Worᴸˡ Mʳ Tho: Rolff.

In addition to her new English religion, Pocahontas took a new English name, Rebecca, and a new English husband, John Rolfe. This portrait was painted when she visited London in 1616 with her husband and young son.

ished in 1591. Our historical mythology makes Pocahontas "The Mother of Us All"—a heroine who blended American-style moxie with feminine, self-sacrificing courage. Little wonder that her image has appeared down through the centuries on everything from ships' figureheads to cigar bands to perfume bottles.

From Pocahontas's perspective, however, the transformation from favored daughter of the Powhatan emperor to savior of the English colonizers could not have been so simple. True, she seems to have gained the gratitude—even the respect—of the English at Jamestown. But did she lose something of her Powhatan self in the process? From 1607 on, Pocahontas would live between two cultures, one English and one—as Smith's people mistakenly called it—"Indian." Among the colonizers and with her father's people, she would continue to serve as a translator of English and Algonquian words. She would also become an important bridge between these two groups, promoting mutual understanding between English and Algonquian worlds. She would help the strangers to flourish in her land. And, at the

In 1613, after being abducted and held captive for months by the Jamestown settlers, Pocahontas converted to Christianity and was baptized into the Church of England.

same time, she would help her people resist annihilation at the strangers' hands.

In April 1613, during yet another period of strife between the Jamestown settlers and their Powhatan neighbors, Virginia's leaders abducted Pocahontas and held her hostage in an attempt to gain a better bargaining position in negotiations with her father. During the long months of imprisonment, Pocahontas renounced the religious traditions of her birth and was christened as a member of the Church of England. Formally baptized into English culture, she took a new English name: Rebecca. She would soon also take an English husband. In April 1614, only days after her release, she married John Rolfe, an English tobacco planter whom she met during her captivity.

Two years later, in June 1616, she journeyed with her husband and their young son to England. During a seven-month stay there, Pocahontas was presented at the court of Queen Anne and honored at palace balls and affairs of state as Lady Rebecca, a symbol of the promise of the "new" world. Observers praised her fluent spoken English and what John Smith called her "very formall and civill . . . English manner." She had become, as he later wrote in his *Generall Historie*, a "gracious lady."

Though they might have celebrated her transformation from Indian princess to Christian woman, her adopted English family was never unaware of her foreignness. Perhaps, then, it is richly symbolic that while in London she stayed with her husband and son at a rooming house called the "Belle Savage Inn." It also seems sadly fitting that the unfamiliar damp cold of London soon proved ruinous to her health. A move to the English countryside alleviated her symptoms, but failed to cure her. Bound at last for her native Werowocomoco (her husband's Virginia) in March 1617, she died of pneumonia or tuberculosis before the ship left the harbor at Gravesend. She was eulogized by an English preacher, buried in English soil, and entombed under her English name.

Pocahontas is the most famous Native American woman to have navigated the rocky path between the Indians' and Europeans' new worlds. But she is certainly not the only one—nor was she the first. In fact, it is possible to identify a Pocahontas-like figure at the center of virtually every major encounter between natives and Europeans from the 15th century through the 19th.

This statue in North Dakota commemorates Sacajawea, the Shoshone woman who traveled across North America as a guide and translator for Meriwether Lewis and William Clark.

Nearly a hundred years before Pocahontas met John Smith, a native woman had played a vital if enigmatic role in the European conquest of Mexico. When Hernán Cortés overthrew the emperor Montezuma and captured the Aztec capital of Tenochtitlan in 1519, he had at his side an Indian woman named Doña Marina or "La Malinche." Marina's skill as a translator of the Nahuatl language made her invaluable to Cortés. It also made her an ambiguous figure among her own people—part emissary and part traitor. Like Pocahontas, La Malinche became the wife of a European and the mother of children who were European *and* Indian (in this case, both Spanish and Aztec). Like Pocahontas, she existed in both of these worlds—and belonged completely in neither one.

Almost three hundred years after Doña Marina became a foremother of the Mexican people, Indian women were still bridging the gaps between Euro-American and Native American worlds. In 1805, the famed Sacajawea, Shoshone wife of a French trader, journeyed across the young United States as part of the expedition led by Meriwether Lewis and William Clark to survey Jefferson's Louisiana Purchase. Like La Malinche and Pocahontas before her, she would serve as their translator, communicating with Shoshone peoples on behalf of the Americans. She would also, like her Aztec and Powhatan forebears, give birth to mixed-race children—children who would cement her dual identity in the American and Shoshone worlds. Thus it is fitting that there are two, conflicting accounts of Sacajawea's end. According to some sources, she died in 1812, still married to her French husband. By this account of the story, she fell victim to a European disease (a "putrid fever," as fur trader John Luttig called it in his diary) in a European outpost (her husband's military camp). Shoshone legend tells a different tale. The Shoshones claim that Sacajawea broke away from her French husband and returned to her native people and her Indian ways on the Wind River reservation. There, they say, she lived to extreme old age, dying in 1884.

Sacajawea's two deaths—like the two *lives* of Powhatan's daughter (first as Pocahontas and then as Lady Rebecca)—serve to illustrate the position in which many native women found themselves during the colonial period. Their stories cannot fully be understood from either the native perspective or the European; rather, their doubled lives reflect their importance to *both* cultures.

Wherever Europeans and native peoples came into contact, Indian women were fundamental links in the chain of mutual exchanges, mutual suspicions, and mutual understandings that bound their two peoples together. Like Pocahontas, native women were not just translators of foreign words. They were also translators of the differences between the so-called "old" and "new" worlds—translators of culture.

This work of "cultural translation" took different forms in different parts of colonial North America. For native women in the Spanish colonies of the Southwest, cultural translation might mean performing one's traditional duties—tasks which typically included childbearing and childrearing; the gathering, serving, and preparing of food; the weaving of blankets and clothing; and the production of pottery—with new materials and for new ends.

Pueblo women used wool from Spanish sheep to increase the production of blankets they had traditionally fashioned from cotton. These wool blankets then became essential for trade with the Spaniards—a trade that cemented the links between the two societies. Similarly, Pueblo women found that the piñon nuts they gathered to add to their families' corn-based diet became, with the arrival of Spaniards, valuable export goods. In almost every facet of women's lives, Pueblo women blended age-old ways with the new

A cloth shirt woven by a Pueblo woman and a coiled basket made by a Zuni woman. The goods produced by Native American women of the Southwest were used in trade with the Spanish.

A Pueblo woman combines the old—the traditional art of basket weaving—with the new—the crosses on the wall, symbols of the Roman Catholic religion brought to the Southwest by the Spanish conquerors.

demands and new materials of the colonial world. Sustenance for both cultures, and harmony between them, were one result of this kind of fusion.

Native women in the American Southwest also engaged—or were *forced* to engage—in another, more literal kind of cultural blending. Like Pocahontas, La Malinche, and Sacajawea, many of them became involved in sexual relationships with European men. All manner of Spanish males, including soldiers, settlers, governors, and even priests, made Pueblo women their sexual partners—often against the women's wills. The rape of native women was a virtual weapon of war for many Europeans trying to bring new territories under their absolute control. Frequent attacks on Indian women were reported by Spanish chroniclers such as Gaspar Castaño de Sosa, who lamented in 1590 that native women "showed very great fear at seeing us" and "wept much" whenever his men entered a village.

Faced with this most violent kind of cultural blending, native women acted not as "translators," but as *resisters* of foreign domination. Amerindian women often spearheaded the opposition to their sexual colonization. In Old California, for example, they led attacks on missions they held responsible for assaults against them. Toypurina, a 24-year-old medicine woman from a settlement near San Gabriel, led the combined forces of six or eight Indian villages in a 1785 attack on the mission there. Confronted with the violence that seemed to go along with the building of the Europeans' "new" world, these native women reasserted the values of their old world.

To be sure, some European men married Indian women, and many extramarital sexual relationships grew out of genuine mutual affection between the partners. The mestizo or mixed people of the colonial Southwest were the offspring of many such unions. But these liaisons between indigenous women and their European colonizers always carried at least the possibility of coercion.

In colonial New France, women from the native groups surrounding the Great Lakes—including the Montagnais-Naskapi, the Cree, the Ottawa, and the Huron—also played dual roles in encounters between their people and the newcomers from across the Atlantic. Where their economic roles were concerned, native women were essential to forging a kind of rapprochement between Indian and European ways. In New France, the chief context for this blending of tradition and innovation was the fur trade. European demand for the fur of beaver, mink, and other animals trapped in America brought subtle transformations to the daily lives of native women in the 17th and 18th centuries. French traders counted on the cooperation of village women who, with seeming enthusiasm, consumed European goods and helped to prepare furs to trade for those goods.

A look at the realm of religion, however, presents a decidedly different picture. Jesuit missionaries—Catholic Frenchmen dedicated to the spiritual conquest of North America—found female natives to be anything but compliant. Particularly in the early 17th century,

Members of the Huron tribe attack Jesuit missionaries. Some Indian tribes fiercely resisted the Jesuits' attempt to convert them to Christianity.

John Winthrop was elected governor of the Massachusetts Bay colony in October 1629 and held the post on and off until his death in 1649.

priests throughout New France accused Indian women of mocking their authority. Even Indian women who did eventually convert were regarded with suspicion. Jesuits accused them of using a thin veneer of Christian practice to conceal a core of traditional beliefs—beliefs they then quietly kept alive within their families. As the colonial period progressed, native women in the Great Lakes region would prove to be fierce guardians of these customary ways.

The varieties of female experience among the hundreds—even thousands—of native North American peoples who first encountered Europeans in the 16th, 17th, and 18th centuries would prove nearly endless. Catawba women in the Carolinas would respond to challenges different from those that the Narragansets confronted in New England. Natchez women in the lower Mississippi Valley would face their own struggles.

And yet, some basic unifying plot lines are visible. Chief among these is a sense of doubleness: of cooperation combined with resistance. Of being a daughter in one culture, a wife in another, and the mother of a third. Of living one's life according to two different sets of beliefs about what women were, should be, *must* be.

The European women who migrated to the North American colonies also knew two worlds. It was in England that women like Margaret Winthrop learned what it meant to be female—and pondered how their roles might change in a strange new world across the Atlantic. Margaret Winthrop was born Margaret Tyndal, daughter of a wealthy landowner in Essex, England. In 1618, at the age of 27, she pledged her love and obedience—along with a substantial dowry of her father's goods and property—to John Winthrop, an aspiring young lawyer from the village of Groton.

John Winthrop had become, by the time he met Margaret, an ardent believer in the growing movement to purge the Church of England of its Catholic, or "popish," practices. He thought of himself as what historians now term a Puritan: one who wished to reform the Anglican faith from within. He did not—at least not at first—wish to remove himself from the "old" world. In the end, though, Winthrop's passion for a godly life would take him far from what he saw as the increasing spiritual corruption of England. As a prolonged economic depression there worsened, and the noose of government repression tightened around Puritan believers, he looked across the Atlantic. The several North American outposts recently established by the New England Company (later the Massachusetts Bay Company) seemed to him to represent the best hope for building a godly community. In May 1629, John Winthrop wrote to Margaret of his dawning belief that Massachusetts would "provide a shelter and a hidinge place for us and ours." By the end of August, they had decided to journey across the ocean.

At the end of that journey, John Winthrop would emerge as a man of great authority—a central figure in the exodus of Puritan families that came to be known as "the Great Migration." Between

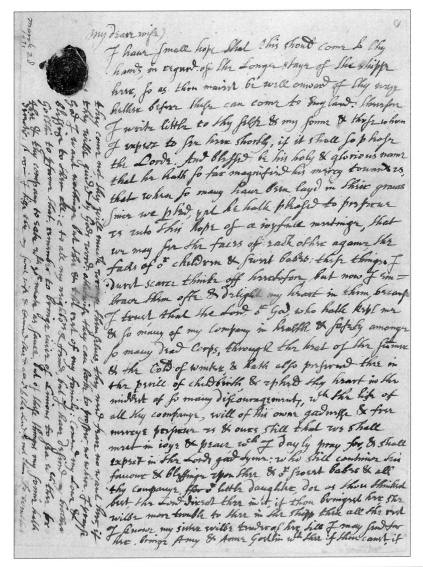

This letter from John Winthrop to his wife Margaret is dated March 28, 1631.

1629 and 1640, some 21,000 English men, women, and children migrated to New England in search of a better life. For most of those years, John Winthrop would rank as a prominent leader. In October 1629, those in charge of the expedition elected him governor of the colony of Massachusetts Bay—an office he continued to hold, off and on, until his death in 1649.

But the migration held a different meaning for Margaret, although she would have to wait more than a year and a half to experience it—and to see her husband again, who journeyed to Massachusetts before her. In some ways, her days in Boston would pass much as they had in Groton, each minute filled with the care of hearth, husband, and children. Her thoughts would most often revolve around the glory of God, much as they had in England. In these ways, her new life would be perhaps no more full of joy than her old one had—nor any less.

In other respects, though, Margaret Winthrop would find her life after 1631 to be quite different. Massachusetts was familiar enough to the Narragansets, Wampanoags, Pequots, Pocomtucs, and Nipmucs who had long made their homes there. But to women like Margaret, it was new indeed. To her, the region's native peoples, along with its forbidding wooded landscape, looked nothing less than "savage." In time, the foreignness of the place and its people would bring about many changes in the ways Margaret Winthrop would work, and love, and pray: changes in the very way she thought. In the end, she would find the life of a woman in this New England to be profoundly unlike what she had left behind—different, and not always easier.

However difficult English women found their first years in New England, other colonial settlements held harder lessons by far. In early Virginia and Maryland, few English women of any rank—fewer still of the elevated status of a Margaret Winthrop—settled until much later in the 17th century. Indeed, the fact that John Rolfe married Pocahontas testifies not only to his lovesickness (as legend has it), but perhaps more directly to the dearth of potential English brides in Jamestown. No females are believed to have been among the "First Supply" of Jamestown settlers in 1607; only two—a gentlewoman and her servant—found their way to Virginia in the "Second Supply" that arrived in the winter of 1608. Well into the 1610s women remained one of Virginia's scarcest and most precious resources.

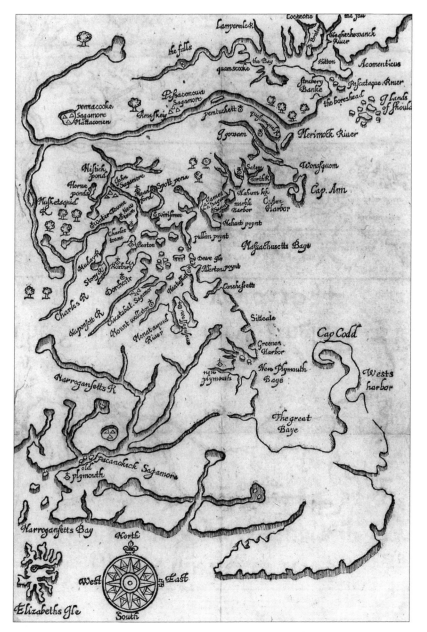

This map of Massachusetts dates from 1634 and is one of the earliest and most detailed maps of the colony.

Starting in November 1619, that colony's leaders undertook a concerted effort to remedy the situation. Sir Edwin Sandys, who was the treasurer of the Virginia Company of London (the group of English investors funding Jamestown), began to recruit women to settle in Virginia. The "want of wives," he wrote, had proved to be among "the greatest of hindrances" to the new plantation. He hoped that the shipment of "an extraordinarily

As this list shows, the first settlers to arrive at the Jamestown settlement in 1607 were all men, most of them young and single.

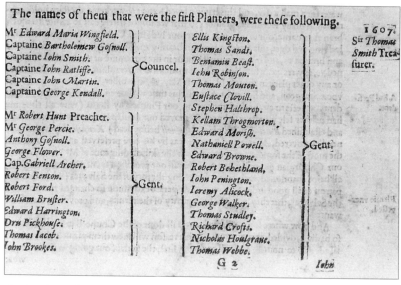

The names of them that were the first Planters, were these following.

1607.
Sir *Thomas Smith* Treasurer.

Mr *Edward Maria Wingfield.*
Captaine *Bartholomew Gosnoll.*
Captaine *Iohn Smith.*
Captaine *Iohn Ratliffe.*
Captaine *Iohn Martin.*
Captaine *George Kendall.*
} Councel.

Mr *Robert Hunt* Preacher.
Mr *George Percie.*
Anthony Gosnoll.
George Flower.
Cap. *Gabriell Archer.*
Robert Fenton.
Robert Ford.
William Bruster.
Edward Harrington.
Dru Pickhouse.
Thomas Iacob.
Iohn Brookes.
} Gent.

Ellis Kingston.
Thomas Sands.
Beniamin Beast.
Iehu Robinson.
Thomas Mouton.
Eustace Clovill.
Stephen Halthrop.
Kellam Throgmorton.
Edward Morish.
Nathaniell Powell.
Edward Browne.
Robert Behethland.
Iohn Penington.
Ieremy Alicock.
George Walker.
Thomas Studley.
Richard Crofts.
Nicholas Houlgraue.
Thomas Webbe.
} Gent.

G 2

Iohn

choice lot of . . . maides" would help "make the men more settled & lesse moveable." According to Sandys's plan, Virginia freemen, desperate for mates, would defray the costs of transporting these "maids." In exchange for 120 pounds of his best tobacco, the man of some means could effectively buy himself a wife. In 1619, 1621, and 1622, a total of nearly 150 English women—most of them young, poor, and alone—ventured across the Atlantic in response to Sandys's campaign. By the end of 1622, every one of them had married. But by 1625, an estimated three-quarters of them were dead of starvation and disease. Similar patterns would be found all over the southern Atlantic coast from Maryland south to the Caribbean.

We know very little about what these first "wives for Virginia" and other women in the colonial South thought of their transplanted lives. In most cases, little beyond their names, their ages, and their places of birth survive in the records. Where a literate, self-reflective Puritan matron like Margaret Winthrop might confess her fears and hopes in letters to her husband, the young women of humble birth who sailed for the Chesapeake were less often able to put their thoughts on paper. They left behind only the most meager data—fragmentary records like lists of passengers on ships leaving England: Jane Dier, 25 years old, widow, departed England 1621; Alice Pindon, aged 19, arrived Viriginia 1635. Little other information about these women has been discovered.

This highly romanticized painting of English settlers landing at Jamestown was painted many years after the fact.

Although there is very scanty evidence of the innermost feelings of these women, we do know that their new world was a particularly difficult—indeed, deadly—place. Recruiters might claim, as William Alsop did in an anonymous pamphlet encouraging female adventurers to come to Maryland, that "women that go over into this Province as Servants, have the best luck as in any place of the world." The real story, however, was not nearly so rosy. The few letters that do survive, including one written by a young Huguenot named Judith Giton who fled the persecution of Protestants in France for the newly settled colony of South Carolina in 1685, speak of unremitting hardship. Since "our arrival in Carolina," she wrote, "we [have] suffered all sorts of evils. . . . sickness, pestilence, famine, poverty, and the roughest labor." In other corners of the early colonial South, Englishwomen's stories were much the same. Seventeenth-century ballads like "The Trappan'd Maiden" set their suffering to music, with verses featuring a "distressed damsel's" lament:

The shortage of women in the colonies led recruiters to resort to trickery and deceit to bring women to America. This song tells the story of a wife whose husband sold her for £10 and sent her to Virginia.

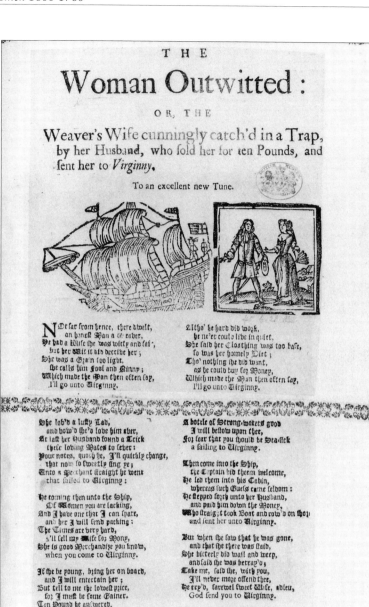

A thousand woes beside, that I do here abide
In the Land of Virginny, O;
In misery I spend my time that hath no end
When that I am weary, weary, weary, O.

"No rest . . . I can have, whilst I am here a Slave." That was the musical complaint of the weary young "Trappan'd Maiden." But, of course, she was not really a slave—not, at least, in the way slavery would soon come to be defined in the Chesapeake. In fact, 1619—the very same year that Edwin Sandys began his drive to enlist wives for Virginia's white men—was the first time Africans would be forced to see North America as their "new" world. Unlike even the poorest settlers who migrated from England, those who made up what the papers of the Virginia Company refer to as the "cargoe of twentie Negroes" that a Dutch ship brought to Jamestown that year did not make the journey by choice. We do not know if any women numbered among those first African Americans, but they followed soon after. And, by the 1660s, it would become increasingly clear that black women and their children would occupy very different places in the social order than their white counterparts did.

As early America took shape, the lives of all of these sorts of women—black and white, native and immigrant, rich and poor—would come to have much in common. As daughters, wives, and mothers, they would share certain expectations and realities where work, love, sex, and even death were concerned. Yet their lives would also be marked by dramatic differences. This blend of sameness and difference in the lives of women in early America becomes visible when we consider the kinds of labor they performed within their various communities.

CHAPTER 2

TO TOIL THE LIVELONG DAY: WORKING LIVES

Samuel de Champlain, a French adventurer-explorer seeking his fortune in New France in the 1610s, thought the native people he encountered there treated their women little better than mules. Huron women, he reported, "have almost the whole care of the house and the work." It was women who "till the soil, sow the Indian corn, fetch wood for the winter"; it was women who "strip the hemp, and spin it." Huron women were also responsible for many other "necessary things"—heavy labor that only the very poorest French matron would ever have been forced to undertake.

French readers of Champlain's dispatches from the New World must have found his descriptions of native women's work rather astonishing. In European villages of the 16th and 17th centuries, women of even modest means typically worked in and around their houses. The good wife, as English minister William Secker was fond of quoting from Proverbs, "looketh well to the ways of her household." Her "trade," as he called housewifery, chiefly concerned "household affairs," especially chores "at the wash-house . . . at the needle, at the wheel," and "at the spindle." She might be required, in a pinch, to lend a hand in the fields. But on a routine basis, such duties fell only to women who found themselves in exceptional cir-

In this family scene from 1664, a Huron woman grinds corn while her baby rests secure, swaddled on a cradleboard nearby.

cumstances: cursed with too few sons to work their land, too poor to hire extra hands, or both.

But in the Huron villages Champlain visited, there *were* no houses to speak of—at least none that *he* considered worthy of that name. Instead, there were dirt-floored "lodges" or "cabins" that one Jesuit preacher described as "a miniature picture of Hell" in which family members "mingled pell-mell with the dogs."

Here women as often as not worked out-of-doors, while Huron men seemed to do relatively little—little, that is, that Champlain recognized as proper, manly labor. Indian husbands, he wrote, "do nothing but hunt deer and other animals, fish, build lodges and go on the war-path." As far as he could tell, native men spent their days in pursuits befitting European gentlemen—hunting and fishing were popular leisure activities for French aristocrats—while their wives toiled.

"Among these tribes are found powerful women of extraordinary stature," Champlain wrote. From his perspective, this was no compliment. As he saw it, the "extraordinary" strength of Huron women was a sign of their nation's primitiveness. To him, the Huron were a people so lacking in civility that they forced women to perform "men's" work while allowing men to perform no work at all.

The French explorer Samuel de Champlain was shocked to see that the men of the Huron tribe did little besides hunt and fish, leaving the bulk of the farming work to the women.

The French settlers of the Great Lakes were not alone in this opinion. All across colonial North America, European observers from a variety of backgrounds reacted with shock to the ways in which native men and women divided up their daily labors. But exactly what do their reactions tell us? They *claim* to tell us what Indian women *did*: that they worked in the fields as well as at their hearths. That their physical burdens were often heavy—*too* heavy, by European standards. When we dig deeper, however, these "Old World" reactions tell us more about European standards than about the ways native peoples divided their daily labors.

Everywhere Europeans looked, the indigenous people they happened upon had their *own* ideas of how men and women should behave. Chief among these were notions about the kinds of work women and men should each perform. These differences were deeply unsettling to the colonists. We today accept that one people can favor a particular kind of social order while another erects a different and equally valid one. But people in 17th-century England, France, Holland, and Spain believed, in contrast, that there was one right way for people to act. From their vantage point, there was an incontestable logic behind the duties men and women were each called upon to perform: the logic of nature, the logic of God. Their sexual division of labor—the ways in which European men and women divvied up their tasks—was understood as much more than a convenient social arrangement. It was, to them, a reflection of the divine plan that made men men, and women women.

Coming to a new world was not supposed to challenge that plan. English migrants in the 17th century were not trying to re-imagine what it meant to be male or female. Instead, these first European settlers hoped their culture and their working lives could be easily transplanted. Immigrant women and men would each perform their customary duties; husbands and wives would find their roles and their relationships appreciably unaltered. Goodwives and yeomen, indentured workers and serving maids, elite "mistresses" and their gentleman partners: each would perform essentially the same duties they had in the Old World. Or would they? The Europeans' New World had its own set of answers in store.

Almost every woman who left England for Virginia or Maryland in the early 17th century would have expected to work—and

Indentured servants signed documents such as this that legally bound them to their masters for a period that could last anywhere from four to seven years. The vast majority of Englishwomen who came to Virginia in the 17th century came as indentured servants.

work hard—from the moment she reached her destination. Between 80 and 90 percent of the English folk who emigrated to that region, and virtually all of the women, came as indentured servants. This meant that the great majority of the anonymous, young, single women who journeyed to the Chesapeake arrived not as free people but as bound laborers, having contracted to work off the cost of their passage by serving for a period of years (typically, from four to seven) in the household of the person who had put up the money for their transport. At first, then, these young women toiled for men who were their masters. After their debts had been satisfied, they might work alongside their husbands on small plantations. In either case, their labors would be shaped by the broader goal of the region's economy: extracting from the soil the maximum possible volume of tobacco, the intoxicating leaf Londoners were craving.

From the first, the speculators who invested in Virginia and Maryland saw their ventures as a potential source of great profit. In the early years in Jamestown they had tried their hands at cultivating silk and unearthing minerals. By the early 1620s, however, it was clear that another product would provide the quickest returns on their investments. Virginia tobacco commanded decent prices from

Tobacco was the crop that fueled the economies of Virginia and Maryland. In this fanciful illustration, a woman is outfitted from head to toe in tobacco leaves.

British merchants—prices high enough to ensure that, for a time, every available acre in the Chesapeake would be devoted to its cultivation. What's more, every available hand—and many more—would be needed to till the soil.

These were the economic necessities that defined the existence of English women in the Chesapeake. Unlike other parts of British America, theirs would not be a world of closely-knit villages and family farms where people grew just enough to get by. Instead, they would find themselves scattered along large tracts of tobacco land, governed by the boom and bust cycles of cash crop agriculture.

Especially while she remained a servant, the environment in which the female immigrant labored meant that prevailing English notions of "women's work" could hardly apply to her. Conditions in the early Chesapeake were mean—even by the standards of those who, like most indentured servants, came from the lower rungs of English society. The average planter was likely to inhabit an unpainted wooden dwelling no larger than 25 by 18 feet—about the size of a modern two-car garage. These so-called "Virginia houses" usually consisted of a single room on the ground floor with some storage space under the eaves above. The first floor "hall" or large room served as the family's kitchen, dining area, workroom, living quarters, and bed chamber; maidservants and children might climb a ladder to sleep on straw pallets in the windowless storage space upstairs. Many servants made do with less, bunking in barns and in outdoor sheds.

The indentured servant's clothing and meals were likely to be as rude as her dwelling place. Her skirts and aprons would have been fashioned of a blend of the coarsest linen and wool. And her diet, as one traveler to the region reported, consisted mainly of a "somewhat indigestible soup" of ground corn. Not surprisingly, serving girls eking out this kind of meager existence often succumbed to the Chesapeake's many endemic diseases. Malaria, pellagra, dysentery, and deadly "agues and fevers" killed off many during the crucial first six months of "seasoning," as getting used to the climate was called. All told, a combination of poverty, deprivation, hunger, and disease insured that, until the last quarter of the 17th century, only a fraction of Englishwomen would outlive their indentures.

This poor planter's house in Maryland was a sparsely furnished, one-room house with a loft. The floors were dirt and the walls were unplastered. Total dimensions measured 20 feet square or less.

Those who did manage to survive these harsh beginnings inherited a world in which women's working lives were dramatically different from what they had been in England. For one thing, the 17th-century Chesapeake was a world in which white women were scarce. Nearly 20 years after the founding of Jamestown, there were still more than three times as many men as women. Because so few Englishmen were able to find wives, and because English migrants continued to die at shockingly early ages, the proportions of men to women—which historians call the "sex ratio"—did not begin to even out until the early 18th century. As late as 1691, there were three Englishmen for every two Englishwomen in Virginia. In Maryland, female immigrants were outnumbered six to one in the 1630s and by as much as three to one from 1650 to 1680.

This imbalance had many implications. On the positive side, it meant that virtually every female migrant would eventually find a husband—should she live long enough to attain her freedom. (Indentured servants, male and female, were forbidden to marry.) But it also meant that English notions of the proper sexual division of labor simply *could* not apply. In a colony where land was abundant and labor was scarce, a certain degree of flexibility regarding one's day-to-day tasks was an absolute necessity. Vast fields were all but begging for hands to plant them. It was almost a foregone conclusion that some of those hands would be women's.

The Chesapeake planter's wife could not afford to center her labors around her house and its surrounding yards. Her work was needed elsewhere. Particularly if she were indentured under or married to the poorer sort of planter, the daily chores of the Englishwoman in Virginia or Maryland were likely to include work in the fields. Incomplete records make good estimates hard to come by, but roughly half of the white women in Maryland and at least that percentage in Virginia would routinely have engaged in heavy agricultural work.

Their specific duties varied with the season. But there was always plenty to do, for tobacco required nearly constant attention.

Growing and harvesting tobacco was a time-consuming, labor-intensive task. This illustration portrays some of the steps involved. In the background, slaves hang tobacco leaves for drying. The woman in front strips the cured tobacco leaves from the plant and packs them into a barrel.

For men and women alike, the workday stretched from sunrise to sunset, with time off during the heat of the day in the warmer months. In the winter—the beginning of the tobacco production cycle—an Englishwoman would have spent those hours helping her master or her husband plant crops and enrich the seedbeds. By late April, she might have been called upon to transplant the tiny seedlings to the main fields—a delicate task that demanded the intensive effort of the whole plantation labor force over a period of several months. In June, July, and August, her deft hands would hoe and weed the tiny hills surrounding each plant and keep the plants free from worms. September brought the arduous labor of cutting and curing the mature leaves; this was typically men's work. But the planter's wife might well lend a hand in the stripping, stemming, curing, and packing that followed later in the fall. By Christmas, the whole cycle was ready to begin again—calling for at least some of her attention at every point in the coming year.

The planter's wife who lived in a more elevated household might have avoided regular outdoor labor. But every white woman in Virginia and Maryland—from the most prominent to the most humble—would have helped to sustain this "tobacco culture" with her daily chores. By preparing food and washing linens, she could free up the men and boys to work outdoors. By tending a vegetable garden on cleared land near her house lot, she could supplement the family's diet and perhaps even make a little cash to pay for imported items like cloth and iron ware—English goods nobody in the Chesapeake had time to produce.

As the century wore on, the planter's wife would have become increasingly enmeshed in informal networks of female trade, swapping her yarn for a neighbor's knitted goods, her butter for some peas. She might also, during especially pressured times, put in long days in the fields. Her working life, then, would represent a kind of hybrid: a blend of Old World expectations and New World realities.

Until the last decades of the 17th century, enough English people saw enough opportunity in the Chesapeake to keep this system limping along. Despite reports about the adversity that awaited them, they kept on coming. But beginning in the 1660s and 1670s, a variety of changes began to overtake the region—changes that made the immigration of indentured English servants both less desirable and less necessary.

A prolonged slump in tobacco prices during the 1680s and 1690s meant fewer opportunities for immigrant laborers. Many would-be migrants chose instead to stay in England, where wages were rising. At the same time, the staggering mortality rates of the colonies' early years were leveling off. White servants who arrived in the 1650s and 1660s more often survived their indentures and became planters in their own right. As more serving girls lived to become planters' wives, and as their children survived to marry and have children of their own, sex ratios drew more nearly equal. By the 1690s, the region's white population was growing by natural increase—a surplus of births over deaths—rather than by immigration.

By the mid 18th century, the labor of the average planter's wife more closely resembled that of her kinswomen back in England than that of her forebears in Virginia and Maryland. Freed from daily chores in the fields, she spent most of her time engaged in such traditionally feminine duties as cooking, sewing, dairying, gardening, tending poultry and hogs, and caring for children. Without electricity, running water, or store-bought goods, this was backbreaking work, but it was probably easier than field work.

What—or, more precisely, *who*—allowed all but the poorest white women in the southern colonies to make this retreat? For the most part, the answer is black women and men. Planters' wives were increasingly able to restrict themselves to duties befitting proper English matrons because they enslaved Africans to do the rest of their work. Shifts in the nature of white women's labor were tied, directly and indirectly, to perhaps the greatest change in the economy and society of the colonial Chesapeake: the rapid growth of race-based, perpetual slavery.

Africans and their descendants had been working the land since a Dutch ship unloaded a group of 20 blacks at Jamestown in 1619. But at first they comprised only a tiny fraction of the region's labor force; as late as 1660 fewer than one-fifth of Maryland's bound laborers were black. And, for most of the 17th century, the status of these forced African immigrants remained ambiguous. Like the white laborers whom they worked alongside, some black workers were servants who survived their indentures to become free men and women. Some eventually owned land, managed their own plantations, hired their own servants, and headed their own families.

An engraving from The Compleat Housewife: or Acomplish'd Gentlewoman's Companion, *published in London in 1750. Only a few wealthy families had such kitchens. Most colonial families made do with much less.*

Before the turn of the 18th century, however, the status of the region's black laborers had changed and their numbers had dramatically increased. By 1700, roughly two-thirds of Maryland and Virginia's bound laborers were black slaves whose perpetual servitude was enforced by law. Further south, in South Carolina, Africans and their descendants comprised a majority of the whole population by 1708.

The conditions under which these involuntary African immigrants lived and labored varied widely, depending on the particular crops they slaved on: tobacco and wheat in the Chesapeake, rice and indigo in the Carolinas, and sugar in the Caribbean. But, as the colonial period wore on, Africans throughout the colonies found their status defined by one thing more than any other: by the color of their skin. Because they were black, their differences from one another became in many ways less significant than their enforced separation from all whites.

At first, few women could be found among the enslaved labor force of the southern colonies. Most 17th-century planters thought that strong male hands made better investments. Until the 1660s, two African men were imported for every African woman. But as white settlers began to turn the servitude of blacks into chattel slavery—a lifelong, even hereditary state—the logic of enslaving more women became clear. Enslaved men could labor only so many hours in the course of a day. But, as the masters saw it, enslaved women were *always* working, even when they were feeding their families or delivering babies. In the loathsome cycle of slavery, African women were perpetual producers: giving birth to more slaves, who could

Under the watchful eyes of their master and his son, slaves work on an indigo farm in South Carolina. Rice and indigo, a valuable blue dye, were the primary crops in the Carolinas.

harvest more crops, the profits from which would provide more capital, which could be used to buy more slaves.

White planters made little distinction between the kinds of work they considered suitable for male and for female slaves. Englishmen might lament that Indian women worked as hard as slaves. But none seemed troubled by making the African women they enslaved work as hard as Indians. An overwhelming majority of African women worked in the fields during the colonial period. As planter Thomas Nairne wrote in his *Letter from South Carolina*, "Hoes, Hatchets Broad Axes, and other necessary Tools" were perfectly appropriate equipment for female slaves. Occasionally a planter might specify, as Virginia's William Fitzhugh did in his will, that a favored female slave "be exempted from working in the ground." But such provisions were clear exceptions; most female slaves between the ages of 10 and 50 could expect to spend the majority of their time working in the fields.

When white women were forced to work out-of-doors, their labor was typically restricted to the less arduous tasks connected with the cultivation of whichever cash crop their region produced. Planters seem to have felt no such compunction where their enslaved female work force was concerned, however. In fact, some evidence suggests that as plantation economies became more complex in the late 18th century, male slaves were diverted to the skilled trades, leaving the heaviest manual labor to their womenfolk.

Slave women deemed incapable of field labor—the very young, the infirm, and the very old—might be put to work in household service. In the first half of the 18th century, these indoor workers accounted for a distinct minority of female slaves, well under 20 percent. And being assigned to the plantation household was not necessarily desirable. Unlike field work, which often took place in gangs of six or more slaves away from the master's watchful eye, housework meant nearly constant supervision and a heightened risk of sexual exploitation as well. And sundown did not mean the end of the house slave's day. Slave women who worked in their mistresses' homes were always on call. Their duties ranged from hard, physical labor like doing laundry and toting water, to such routine drudgery as emptying chamber pots and making beds. That English people considered such tasks appropriately "feminine" was very much beside the point; housewifery took on a very different meaning when performed under compulsion for people who claimed to own both you and your offspring.

Slave women demonstrated their hatred for the hardships and injustices of their working lives through courageous acts of resistance to their owners' demands. Sometimes, a woman's challenge to her enslavement might take a passive form. Virginia planter Landon Carter, for example, wrote in his diary about Mary, who escaped field work by faking "fits"; Sarah, who managed to extract *11* months of reduced work assignments because of an overlong pregnancy; and

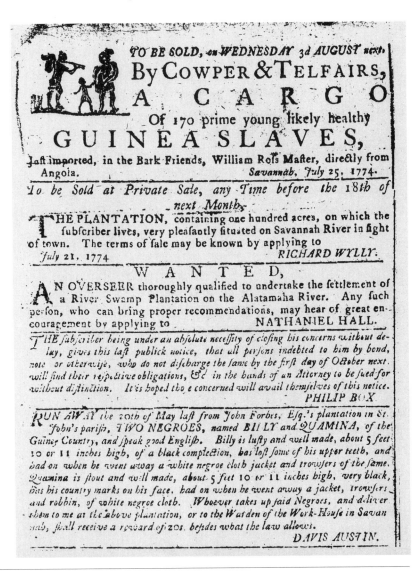

The top of this broadside is an advertisement for a slave auction to be held in Savannah, Georgia. At the bottom of the broadside, a slave owner posts a reward for the return of two slaves who were courageous enough to run away.

Wilmot, who regularly "pretended to be too heavy [with child] to work." Such strategies enraged planters. But for slave women they bought precious extra time—time for tending the small gardens that nourished their families; time to spend caring for their children instead of waiting on their master's kin.

Other African-American women rebelled in more violent ways. They ran away. They murdered masters who raped them. They refused the whip. They burned down the houses in which they were forced to toil. In 1755, a female slave whose name we do not know was burned at the stake in Charleston for poisoning her master—an act that must have raised fear among all the whites who enslaved black women to work in their kitchens.

In the southern colonies, then, "women's work" meant many things. English folks had distinct ideas about the labor women *should* do. But the work women actually *did*—whether they were Powhatans, planters' wives, indentured servants, or African slaves—was a different matter altogether. Regardless of whether the crop in question was tobacco or rice, corn or sugar or indigo, the urgency of farming crops for export often outweighed notions of proper feminine behavior.

Seventeenth-century New England was the destination of a very different sort of English migrant than the restless young adventurers who sailed to the Chesapeake. Seeking primarily to set up independent, pious communities rather than to turn a quick profit, many of those who settled in the colonies of Massachusetts Bay, Plymouth, New Haven, Connecticut, and Rhode Island were looking for a new way of life: one in which God-fearing folk could band together in communities organized for their collective good in this world and the next. In many ways, however, their new lives would resemble the ones they left behind. For these were migrants who brought with them as much of Old England as they possibly could.

One of the most important ways in which New England mirrored Old was in the age structure and sex ratio of its population. More than 85 percent of those who came over during the 1630s brought along at least their immediate kin. The predominance of families, coupled with what, in contrast to the Chesapeake, were relatively healthy living conditions, created communities that were able to reproduce themselves by natural increase almost from the start.

Once a woman reached New England and was married, she was encouraged to start having babies to boost the population of the colonies.

Later in the 17th century, variations on this pattern of immigration would be found in many areas within the so-called "middle colonies" which lay between New England and the Chesapeake. As late as 1660, the region stretching from northern New York to the lower Delaware Bay held fewer than 6,000 white settlers of diverse European origins. Dutch merchants, farmers, and fur traders predominated in New Netherland, where they lived in trading centers like New Amsterdam (later Manhattan) and remote rural outposts like the borough of Rensselaerswyck, which included Albany. Further to the south, Dutch settlers competed with Swedish and Finnish migrants for title to the rich lands along the Delaware River.

Beginning in the mid-1660s, when the English crown seized control of the region, these small settlements embarked on a period of rapid growth. With soil more fertile than New England's and a climate less noxious than the Chesapeake's, the colonies of New York (the English name for New Netherland, forcibly annexed from the Dutch in 1664), New Jersey (1664), and Pennsylvania (1682) proved ideal for the production of different types of grains—especially wheat. Reports of the good living to be made there, along with the promise of greater religious tolerance than was the norm in most other places, soon attracted large numbers of migrants from England, Scotland, Wales, Ireland, Switzerland, and Germany as well as from other parts

of British America. By 1700, the region was one of the fastest growing and most ethnically diverse in all of British America, with a population of more than 50,000 white inhabitants, a sizable number of
slaves, and a growing community of free blacks.

More than half of the white settlers who flocked to New Jersey
and Pennsylvania in the late 17th and early 18th centuries came in
family groups. But ships' passenger lists also reveal that a sizable
number of young, unmarried male servants sought their fortunes in
the middle colonies. As a consequence, men outnumbered women in
the early years of white settlement, though never by as much as they
did further to the south.

The presence in New England and the middle colonies of a broader
range of English people than could be found in the Chesapeake (there
were children along with adults, women in numbers nearly equal to
men, the middling ranks of yeomen and artisans side by side with
poorer servants and higher-ranking leaders) made it easier for white
settlers in those regions to import English ways. Young couples with
some children already born and more on the way formed the core of
a rapidly growing society that quickly replicated the customs of the
world they had left behind. Ideas about the proper nature of women's
work were one set of English traditions that adapted almost effort-
lessly to conditions in these parts of the "new" world.

Thomas Baily and his wife, heads of the large family that inhabited a three-room house on a 150-acre farm in Chester County, Penn-

*This 19th-century view of a
17th-century kitchen shows
three generations of a family
working and living under one
roof—an unusual arrangement.*

sylvania, in the 1760s, were average in many respects. Like most people in their corner of the middle colonies, they planted wheat, rye, and barley and raised some livestock on the side. Where the aim of the Chesapeake planter's household was to produce as much as possible—as much tobacco, as much cash, as many slaves—the goal of the family was, more often, to produce just enough. Instead of striving to get ahead, the Bailys and people like them thought in terms of subsisting, of maintaining, of holding on to their position in the world. The harvest from their fields, along with the wool produced by their 24 sheep and the cheese and butter Thomas's wife made from the milk of their five cows, would put food on the table and a bit of cash in their pockets. If Thomas, his wife, their several children, and their servants all worked hard throughout the summer and fall, they could set aside enough dried grains and cured meats in their second-floor storage space to see the family through the winter till the ground was fit for planting again.

Many of "Goody" (short for Goodwife) Baily's duties remained the same throughout the year. On a typical morning, her first waking moments would be spent starting the cooking fires that would smolder throughout the day. Next she might see to the milking, setting aside pans of fresh milk for cream to form. Later, she would churn this cream into butter, salt it, and pack it into wooden molds for storage or sale. After heating up a breakfast of leftovers, she might spend the bulk of her morning preparing food for the day ahead: making a one-dish "pottage" and baking the coarse bread her family would eat at noonday dinner and evening supper, and brewing the beer that accompanied virtually every meal. The majority of the afternoon might be taken up with weeding the garden, washing and mending clothes, or taking grain to the miller's. And, on top of these regular chores, she would have to steal time for her various seasonal tasks: raising calves in the spring; processing milk into cheese, making sausage, and preserving bacon in the summer; putting up preserves in the fall; and completing the seemingly endless duties connected with cloth production (such as carding and spinning the wool she would send out to be woven into coarse fabric) while her garden lay fallow in the winter.

"This day is forty years since I left my father's house and come here, and I have seene little else but hard labor and much sorrow. . . .

This 1780 print, Wethersfield Girls Weeding Onions, *shows a mother and her daughters at work in their garden. For most women during the colonial era the work was never ending.*

I am dirty and tired almost to death." Mary Cooper, the woman who found time to pen these plaintive lines in her diary before retiring late one night in 1769, lived on a family farm in Oyster Bay, New York. Though she lived several hundred miles from Goody Baily, their lives had much in common. Cooper, too, spent her days cooking and washing and preserving and sewing and marketing and trading.

Indeed, with subtle variations, almost *any* woman in colonial America might have made these comments. Had the writer been a black slave in the Chesapeake, we might imagine, she could not have "left her father's house" of her own free will. If she were an indentured white servant in Maryland, she might well not have even *survived* forty years after marriage. If she were a very wealthy woman in New England, the Carolinas, Pennsylvania, or Virginia, she might have been just a little less dirty and felt just a bit less tired. But regardless of her race, region, or status, the central fact of nearly endless toil would have marked the lives of all of these women.

The Well-Ordered
FAMILY:
OR,
Relative DUTIES.

BEING THE
Substance of several SERMONS,

About {
Family Prayer.
Duties of *Husbands & Wives.*
Duties of *Parents & Children.*
Duties of *Masters & Servants.*
}

By Benj. Wadsworth. A.M
Pastor of a Church of CHRIST in Boston, N.E.

Psal ci.2.7.— *I will walk within my house with a perfect heart.*— *He that worketh deceit, shall not dwell within my house* ——

Josh. xxiv. 15. *As for me and my house, we will Serve the Lord.*

Gen. xviii. 19. —— *He (that is, Abraham) will command his Children and his houshold after him, and they shall keep the way of the Lord.*

BOSTON: Printed by B. Green, for *Nicholas Butsolph,* at his Shop in Corn-Hill. 1712.

CHAPTER 3

OF MARRIAGE AND MOTHERHOOD: FAMILY LIVES

I t was during the fall of 1664 that Martha Cross first realized the extent of her dilemma. This young woman from the godly village of Ipswich, Massachusetts, found herself in a decidedly un-Puritan situation: She, as yet unmarried, was going to have a baby. What was even worse was that the father of the child, one William Durkee, did not seem particularly interested in sharing his future with her. Indeed, as Martha's sister later told the Essex County magistrates, Durkee had gone so far as to say that "he had rather keep the child than keep her!" In time, Durkee retracted these cruel words, telling Martha that "if he kept one he would keep the other." But the promise seemed lukewarm at best. No wonder Martha felt, as her sister reported, "in sore distresse of mind."

Living in an era during which marriage was an unquestioned norm, abortion was risky at best, and single parenthood was all but unheard of, Martha Cross did not know what to do. She talked the matter over first with the women among whom she spent her working days: her sister and several female neighbors. Then, like the dutiful daughter she had always been, she sought counsel from the most important man in her life—one whose opinion mattered even more than Durkee's—her father.

Robert Cross's reaction did not make matters any easier. News of his daughter's transgression plunged him, neighbors told the court,

The title page of a 1712 collection of sermons given by Benjamin Wadsworth in Boston. People looked to the clergy for guidance on the duties of husbands and wives, parents and children, and masters and servants.

into "a sad and sorrowfull Condition" and he found himself unsure "which way to turn or what to say." Martha, her sister, and two neighborhood women impressed upon him their sense of the best possible resolution: that he should allow his frantic daughter to marry the wretched Durkee. By tradition, this was his decision to make. Martha was his to give in marriage—and his to withhold.

For reasons we do not know, Cross chose the latter course. Perhaps, struck by reports of Durkee's less-than-enthusiastic proposal, Robert Cross thought Martha deserved better. Perhaps, like many fathers of his era, he wished to retain some vestige of control over his adult children. Perhaps he worried about the fate of Martha's older sisters. If she married before them, would they seem less desirable to potential suitors? Whatever the reasons behind the decision, however, Cross's wishes soon became moot. His verdict in the matter was overruled by the county magistrates, who, fearful of becoming responsible for the financial support of a fatherless infant, allowed Martha and William to marry before their child was born.

Martha Cross's situation was, to be sure, an unhappy one. But in many respects it was not an unusual one—not even in Massachu-

Ashley Bowen drew this illustration of his unsuccessful courtship of Dorothy Chadwick. "Will thee Consent to be my bride?" he asks. She answers, "Sir, I have not that Desirde [desire]."

setts Bay, which was known as the "Bible Commonwealth" because of its strict adherence to Old Testament notions of morality. Courtship, marriage, love, sex, pregnancy, motherhood: These were central experiences shared by all young women in colonial North America. Facets of what we think of as private life, they were not nearly so private in the colonial period. Getting married, having sex, giving birth, and raising children were parts of a woman's life about which her wider community—from her parents, to her siblings, to her neighbors, to the magistrates and ministers who presided over her town— would have something to say.

The particular sequence of steps (from affection to intercourse to marriage to motherhood) might differ according to a woman's race, her region, her religion, her social status—even something as individual as her personality. Thus the headstrong Martha Cross transposed what her father considered to be the proper order of things by becoming pregnant first, seeking his permission second, getting married third, and giving birth within a couple of months. Yet despite the inversion of the initial stages of this progression, the cycles of Martha's life would unfold in ways that had much in common with her female neighbors in New England, with white and

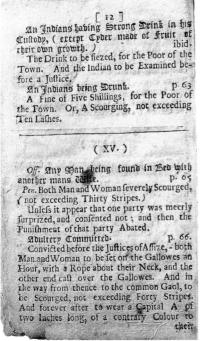
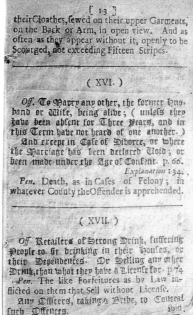

The so-called "Scarlet Letter Law" in 17th-century Massachusetts required those convicted of adultery to wear the letter A sewn on their clothes. It was only one example of the laws the Puritans enacted in an effort to regulate private behavior to conform to God's laws.

black women in the Chesapeake, even with the Native American women whom the English founders of Ipswich had displaced. Just as the seasons of the year governed the working lives of women in various corners of the colonial mosaic, the seasons of the female life course—the biology of sexual maturation, reproduction, and aging—governed the lives of early American women.

Adolescence was the spring of a young woman's life. During their teenage years and into their early twenties, girls in colonial America grew to womanhood, learning what it meant to be wives and mothers in their communities. The progression was a gradual one, because most of the boundaries that separate youth from adulthood in our day would have been meaningless to the typical colonial daughter.

Education, for example, now provides an important measure of maturity. To us, starting kindergarten or graduating from high school are events that symbolize the transition from infancy to childhood to adulthood. But in the colonial period few common people, and still fewer girls of any social class, received much formal education. In the Puritan colonies, civil authorities deemed knowledge of the Bible so important that they passed laws requiring that children attain basic literacy. Taught by their parents, by the head of the household in which they served as apprentices, or, increasingly after 1690, in a "dame school" that convened in the home of a local woman during slack periods of the agricultural year, most boys and girls probably

This 17th-century slate alphabet board was used to teach boys and girls to read. Usually, only boys were taught to write. By the late 18th century, most children went at least part-time to "dame schools," run by local women.

learned how to read. *Writing*, however, was considered a separate skill (even an art), one reserved primarily for boys. Some local laws made the distinction official by proclaiming that boys should learn to read, write, and cipher (do math) while girls should master reading and needlework.

Not surprisingly, then, a wide gap separated male and female rates of literacy in colonial America. In mid-17th-century New England, roughly 60 percent of white men could write well enough to sign their names on a will; only 30 percent of Anglo-American women could. Over time both male and female literacy increased. But so, too, did the gap between them. As late as 1775, when nine out of ten white men in the region could write, less than half of New England's white women had the same degree of skill. The gap would not be closed until the second quarter of the 19th century. Throughout the North American colonies, girls' education lagged behind their brothers'. Variations on this general pattern could be found among people of different social classes. Daughters of the colonial elite, for example, received more schooling than their poorer counterparts. Unlike their brothers, however, wealthy girls rarely learned Greek and Latin and never attended college.

Rates of female schooling and literacy also varied by region. Girls living in towns generally received more education than the daughters of rural farmers. Thus young women in New England generally fared better than those in the Chesapeake, where the relative lack of settled towns and the absence of a strong religious motivation for reading made female education a haphazard proposition. Fewer than 20 percent of non-elite women in Virginia could sign their names. In the Dutch colony of New Netherland, in contrast, an economy based on commerce made knowing how to read and write essential. There, literacy was widespread for men and women alike. Although boys typically received more schooling than their sisters, most girls learned the rudiments of reading, writing, and math. In the late 17th century, an estimated 80 percent of men and 75 percent of women in New Netherland could write.

Wherever they lived, Euro-American girls had a much better chance of learning to read and write than their Native American and African-American counterparts did. In Puritan New England as well as in the Catholic settlements of New France and the Spanish border-

In *Adam's* Fall
We Sinned all.

Thy Life to Mend
This *Book* Attend.

The *Cat* doth play
And after flay.

A *Dog* will bite
A Thief at night.

An *Eagles* flight
Is out of fight.

The Idle *Fool*
Is whipt at School.

As runs the *Glaſs*
Mans life doth paſs.

My *Book* and *Heart*
Shall never part.

Job feels the Rod
Yet bleſſes GOD.

Our *KING* the
good
No man of blood.

The *Lion* bold
The *Lamb* doth hold.

The *Moon* gives light
In time of night.

Nightingales ſing
In Time of Spring.

The *Royal Oak*
it was the Tree
That ſav'd His
Royal Majeſtie.

Peter denies
His Lord and cries.

Queen *Eſther* comes
in Royal State
To Save the JEWS
from diſmal Fate.

Rachel doth mourn
For her firſt born.

Samuel anoints
Whom God appoints.

Time cuts down all
Both great and ſmall.

Uriah's beauteous Wife
Made *David* ſeek his
Life.

Whales in the Sea
God's Voice obey.

Xerxes the great did
die,
And ſo muſt you & I.

Youth forward ſlips
Death ſooneſt nips.

Zacheus he
Did climb the Tree
His Lord to ſee.

lands, schools for native children—when they existed at all—were typically directed toward transforming "savage" Indians into "civilized" Christians. In this sense, Indian girls and boys paid a heavy price for their schooling. Formal education for African-American slaves was virtually nonexistent, especially in the South, where less than 1 percent of blacks of either sex could read and write. In New England, where the population of slaves and free blacks remained small, black children might receive some rudimentary schooling by attending classes along with their white neighbors. Later in the colonial period, Pennsylvania's Quaker leaders would do more to promote education for African Americans, including opening a school especially for black children in Philadelphia in 1758.

Most of a young woman's training would take place not in any classroom but within her own home, at her mother's side. Beginning by assisting with the care of her younger siblings, she would learn to relieve her mother of such time-consuming tasks as washing and spinning. Eventually, she would grow to fuller competence in hearth and home, becoming an apprentice housewife much as her brother might become an apprentice cobbler or carpenter. Becoming a woman did not require her to forge her own path. Instead, adulthood meant following her mother's path.

An important part of the slow, almost imperceptible transition from girlhood to womanhood was the dawning of sexual maturity. Despite a prevailing belief among Anglo Americans that premarital intercourse was a grievous sin (in New England "fornication"—sex between two unmarried people—was a crime), youth was a time of sexual exploration for many women. Experimentation often led to pregnancy, marriage, and motherhood in quick succession. As many as one in ten New England women were, like Martha Cross, pregnant when they reached the altar. This was only half the proportion that would have been found in England at the time; the watchfulness of neighbors, parents, and authorities saw to that.

Had she lived in the early Chesapeake, Martha Cross would have found even more company in her lamentable condition. The scarcity of women in that region meant that every young girl had plenty of opportunities (and faced plenty of pressures) in matters of the heart. The existence of a Virginia law punishing "dissolute masters" who "have gotten their maides with child" tells us that female

Girls sewed samplers to practice needlework. Some local laws proclaimed that boys should master reading, writing, and arithmetic, while girls needed to master reading, needlework, and other household arts.

servants may have been particularly vulnerable to sexual exploration—and exploitation. In Charles County, Maryland, roughly one-fifth of all the maidservants who arrived from England between 1658 and 1705 were eventually charged with bastardy, the crime of bearing a child out of wedlock. Many of them, the courts found, had been made pregnant by their masters. Thousands of miles from their families back in England, isolated on small plantations, impoverished adolescent girls were easy prey for aggressive or unscrupulous men.

In other ways, though, these young women were also unusually free to make their own choices. Out of necessity, they exercised a degree of control over their lives and their bodies that would have been quite alien to the likes of Ipswich's Martha Cross. Without fathers and mothers to decide their fates (even women born in Virginia and Maryland were often orphaned before they reached their teens), they would have received little guidance about how to direct their affections. But unlike Martha, they did not need anyone's permission. It seems unsurprising, then, that more than one-third of white women in the early Chesapeake were pregnant at the time of

The New England Primer (opposite) used rhymes to help children learn to read. Rhymes such as "The Idle Fool / Is whipt at School" were sure to grab the attention of students and reinforce Puritan ideals of proper behavior.

This 1721 engraving, To-bacco, Cupid's Aid, *claims that tobacco enhances sexual desire and performance.*

their weddings. All told, virtually everyone in the colonial period, whether they lived in a small town like Ipswich or worked on a plantation near the James River in Virginia, miles from their nearest neighbor, would have known young women who became mothers almost as soon as they became wives—if not before.

They would also, undoubtedly, have been acquainted with many more adolescent girls who experimented sexually before marriage but, miraculously escaping pregnancy, were able to keep their dalliances secret. Especially in the densely settled towns of New England, young couples seeking a bit of time alone faced a tough time of it. Houses were small and crowded. Windows were low to the ground, affording easy access to prying eyes. Indeed, privacy as a concept was all but nonexistent; family members, neighbors, and town "fathers" considered it a religious and social duty to monitor even the most intimate goings-on. Still, as Martha's case and so many others show, young women and men who were persistent, clever, and bold enough found chances to steal away on their own. In a world where somebody else always seemed to be nearby, even a few moments alone could be precious.

Although moments of intimacy might be hard to come by, for the most part ordinary young women—those of Martha Cross's middling status or below—found it relatively easy to follow their hearts. A stubborn father might threaten to withhold his consent. But, in the end, such women had considerable say in choosing their mates. Blessed with little in the way of property or status, they had only themselves to offer in marriage. Poverty tended to reduce courtship to its essentials: affection, desire, proximity, convenience, necessity.

For women in the colonial elite, however, adolescence was a different sort of business altogether. Those of at least modest wealth knew that courtship was much more than a flirtation between young lovers. It was, more centrally, the beginning of a connection between families: an arrangement for transmitting property from one generation to the next.

John Winthrop and Margaret Tyndal, transplanted New Englanders of elevated social standing, knew that love and romance were inseparable from duty and property. In a letter he sent her in 1618, John Winthrop's father assured his future daughter-in-law that his son would "always be a most kinde and lovinge husband unto you."

The elder Winthrop also emphasized that his son would be "a provident steward" in Margaret's financial affairs, providing handsomely for her and their children "during his lyfe, and also after his deathe." The Winthrops' marriage, like their courtship, would be part heartfelt affection and part iron-clad contract.

William Byrd II, an aristocratic planter who made his home in early-18th-century Virginia, also knew these two sides of love. In a letter he wrote to his intended, Lucy Parke, while she was away visiting relatives in 1705, he likened the couple to turtle doves who "abound with expressions of tenderness to one another." In a letter to Lucy's father written the same year, Byrd spoke of his "respect and tenderness" for her. But he also took pains to add that his "fortune may be sufficient to make her happy"—especially when coupled with the substantial portion of her father's goods and property which Lucy would undoubtedly bring to the marriage as her dowry.

From Boston to Virginia, courtship among the colonial elite had much in common. It was a ritual dance with a fixed order to its steps. Parents, especially fathers, choreographed the minuet while their sons took a leading role in its performance. Among the elite, women were followers in the complicated "business" of marriage. Their hopes and desires often took a back seat. Affection, too, was

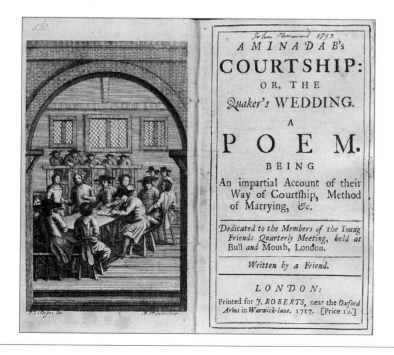

The title page and adjoining woodcut of Aminadab's Courtship, *a satirical poem published in 1717 that poked fun at the elaborate courtship rituals of the Quakers.*

When William Byrd II (1674–1744) a wealthy Virginia planter, was courting his future wife, he assured her father that his fortune was enough to make his daughter happy. Such assurances were necessary among the families of the colonial elite.

of secondary concern. In an ideal situation, love would follow marriage. It did not necessarily have to precede it.

Regardless of the path that brought her there, virtually every woman in 17th- and 18-century America eventually married. The wedding itself might take many different forms. In New England, couples were required to make formal contracts of "espousal" declaring their engagement and then to announce their intentions in the meetinghouse on three separate occasions. Among the Pueblo and Zuni peoples of the Southwest, an exchange of blankets and corn symbolized a couple's union. For wealthier English colonists, a written contract would typically spell out the property consequences of the match in minute detail; for humbler sorts spoken promises would suffice.

A variety of authorities might preside over this exchange of vows, but the ceremony was almost always a small one, typically celebrated in the bride's home. In New England, where marriage was a civil matter, a magistrate was the necessary official; in the Chesapeake, ministers of the Church of England were the celebrants of choice. And, where the authorities needed to solemnize the affair were lacking altogether, many couples must have adopted planter Giles Tomkinson's logic. Brought to court for the crime of bastardy in 1665, he explained to the magistrates of Charles County, Maryland, that he and his wife *were* married and their child, therefore, was legitimate. "To matrimony is only necessary the parties' Consent and . . . a lawfull Churchman," Tomkinson said. If no "churchman" could be found consent alone would have to do.

African-American couples had only their mutual consent to offer. Except in Massachusetts, where a law permitting marriage between slaves was passed in 1705, the unions of black men and women were legitimized neither by law nor by religious leaders in the British colonies. By the mid-18th century, sex ratios among the black population had leveled off enough to allow more slaves to find mates. But despite the unwavering commitment many slave men and women demonstrated toward their families, the bonds between husband and wife, like those between parents and child, were fragile. Masters could—and often did—sell one partner in a marriage, dissolving what was meant to be a lifelong partnership. Whatever its particular conventions, a wedding marked the start of what we might call the summer

This engraving, Marriage of 12 Colonial Couples, *is from an album of Moravian history from the 1750s. In Moravian communities in North Carolina, marriages had to be approved by the board of church elders.*

of a woman's life. It was during her time as a married woman that she would see the lessons planted in adolescence grow to maturity and bear fruit. It was during this season of her life that she would assume the roles of an adult woman: most centrally, those of wife and mother. She would learn to fit her daily chores around the nearly constant childbearing and childrearing that would continue until she reached menopause in her mid to late forties.

This second season of womanhood began at different ages for women living in different parts of the colonial mosaic. In New England, most women had reached their early 20s before they married for the first time. In the Chesapeake, a more complicated pattern held sway. For women like Elizabeth Montague, who came to Virginia from England in the early 1650s, marriage had to wait until the end of a lengthy indenture. Many women of her generation were thus over 25 years old by the time they were free to wed. Their daughters did much to reverse this pattern in a single generation. If they were lucky enough to survive childhood, they were sure to be surrounded by potential suitors. And, with no indentures to satisfy, they had no reason to delay their choice. Elizabeth Montague's youngest daughter and namesake was one such girl. Married in 1671, she was only in her mid-teens.

What did becoming a wife mean for a mere girl like Elizabeth Montague? For one thing, marriage meant a change of residence.

All but the poorest young couples throughout British America followed the English custom of setting up their own, separate households rather than the Native American tradition of residing in a multi-generational dwelling with one's maternal or paternal kin. In Elizabeth's case, the move was delayed by poverty. Her husband, Doodes Minor, and his family were not planters in their own right but tenants who rented a plot of land from Elizabeth's father. At first, she and her husband lived with her in-laws. In time, the hardworking young Doodes scraped together enough profits from this land to allow him to purchase 650 acres for the couple to farm. There Elizabeth would learn the business of being the mistress of her own humble home.

It was not an easy task, but she had to master it quickly, for in rapid succession, she gave birth to six children. Families of this size and larger would have been common in Elizabeth's world. The woman who survived her childbearing years (most in the Chesapeake did not) would have delivered, on average, eight or nine children over the course of her reproductive life. As many as 12 or 13 live births were not unheard of. If Elizabeth followed the typical pattern, she would have given birth to her oldest child within 15 months of her wedding. Thereafter, a new baby would likely follow every two years

Captain and Mrs. Johannes Schuyler, by John Watson, painted in about 1725. Shown standing above his seated wife, Captain Schuyler exemplifies the colonial ideal of male authority in marriage.

or so. Starting a scant year after her marriage, she would spend much of the remainder of her life performing the manifold duties of a housewife—the cooking, the spinning, the dairying, the hog-tending—while either pregnant, nursing, caring for an infant, or all three.

Not only ceaseless labor, but a measure of sadness also came to mark Elizabeth Montague Minor's days. She lived to bury half of her offspring; only three of them survived long enough to bear children of their own. Almost inconceivably tragic in our day, such a family history would have been commonplace in hers. Throughout the 1600s, roughly one-quarter of the children born in the Chesapeake died before their first birthdays; fewer than half reached the age of 20. New England proved much healthier: nine out of ten infants born there survived at least until age five, and perhaps three-quarters lived to see adulthood. Still, in the early modern world the loss of a child was a regular part of a woman's life.

So, too, was the death of a spouse. Elizabeth lost Doodes while she was still a young woman—a fate she may have found heartbreaking but hardly surprising. In the disease-ridden environment in which she lived, either husband or wife was likely to die within seven years of marriage. Of course, with so few women around, widows like Elizabeth did not stay widows long. She remarried quickly, not once but twice. In the end, Elizabeth Montague Minor Cocke Blaze outlasted three husbands. Living out her remaining days on her third husband's plantation, she was positively ancient by Virginia standards. When death came in 1708, she was about 52 years old.

We know a good deal about what women like Elizabeth Montague *did*, but very little about how they *felt*. Was she "in love" with her first husband (or, for that matter, with her second, or her third)? Did her husbands and her children consider her a figure of authority? Or did she remain constantly under the shadow of the man of the house—whoever he was at the moment? The records offer very little in the way of direct answers to such questions. Undoubtedly, Elizabeth Montague would soon have discovered that the mistress of a colonial household occupied a rather precarious rung on the ladder of authority that structured her society. In a world in which the principle of hierarchy was unquestioned—where it was simply assumed that some would always rule from above while others would

Register

Of Samuel Colton's Family He was Born September 7th 1724 & Married Flavia Colton She was born August 31 1741 & by her hath the following Child. viz.

NAMES	BORN	DIED
Nameless child	February 1st 1760	February 3d 1760
Flavia the mother died April 6 1763. Samuel Colton married again October 16th 1765 to Lucy Colton She was born June 24 1742 and by her had the following children		
Adna	August 31 1767	Sept 9 1767
Still Born	November 20 1768	
Flavia	October 1 1769	August 15 1815
Margaret	Nov 18th 1770	December 28 1770
Margaret	October 19th 1771	Jan 7 1817
Lucy	June 8 1773	October 18 1804
Samuel	Sept. 8 1775	August 25 1777
Samuel	Feb 4 1778	June 11 1811

Flavia was married October 11 1787 to Col Alexander Field
Margaret was married September 11 1794 to David Booth
Lucy was married January 29 1794 to Dr Benjamin Stebbins
Samuel was married March 6 1799 to Anne Gregory Barrines

Mr Samuel Colton DIED November 5 1784
Mrs Lucy Colton DIED December 7 1799

serve dutifully below them—the goodwife had to occupy both places at once. As mother and mistress, she would learn to be a ruler of sorts. As wife, however, young Elizabeth Montague Minor was more clearly a subordinate. Her marriage vows would have included pledges to "obey" and "serve" her husband—promises he was not asked to make to her. Doodes Minor, for his part, was supposed to support his wife, to live with her in harmony, to have sex with her alone, and to refrain from physically abusing her beyond the bounds of necessary "correction." He was not, however, expected to "obey" her: to set her word above his own.

The woman's vow of submission in marriage expressed a view of the world that imagined man to be superior and woman to be inferior in almost every respect. Many English writers of the day referred to women as "the weaker vessel," a phrase denoting a being with less intellectual ability, less physical capacity, and less moral fortitude than a man. This notion of female inferiority manifested itself in a variety of ways in colonial America, most centrally through strictures applied by custom, by religion, and by law.

In Elizabeth Minor's day, the shortage of women meant that husbands and wives shared authority more equally than they would

The birth register of Samuel Colton's family of Long-meadow, Massachusetts (left). After the death of his first wife, Flavia, in 1763, Colton took another wife, Lucy, in 1765. Together they had seven children, but only four of them lived past their first year.

John Purves & Wife, Anne Prichard *by Henry Benbridge, painted in about 1775.*

Margaret Mitchell Sewall, shown in her widow's weeds, standard attire for widows in the 18th century. She bore 17 children, several of whom gained positions of prominence in Massachusetts.

later in the colonial period. According to the ancient traditions of the English common law, a wife was entitled only to her "dower thirds"—one-third of her husband's real property—if he died before she did. But many men in the 17th-century Chesapeake went further than the law required, bequeathing at least half their estates to their wives. With no brothers or fathers nearby who might be entrusted with the family's care, these early planters left their widows in control. In terms of married women's property rights as in many other aspects of life, the early Chesapeake was marked by flexibility in the face of necessity.

By the 18th century, however, increased reliance on the English common law imposed narrower strictures on women throughout British America. Published in London in 1765, English jurist William Blackstone's four-volume compendium entitled *Commentaries on the Laws of England* gave precise definition of a wife's legal rights. Blackstone defined the married woman as a woman literally "covered" by her husband's authority. Her "very being or legal existence," he wrote, was "consolidated into that of her husband; under whose wing, protection, and cover, she performs everything." Unless her husband signed a special document permitting her to do so, a married Anglo-American woman could not own or buy property in her own name, enter into a contract, or write a will.

In the colony of New York, one legacy of the early years of Dutch control was a very different set of traditions concerning the rights of married women. Long after the English conquest of New Netherland in 1664, Dutch custom, rooted primarily in Roman civil law rather than in the English common law, governed women's lives. Roman-Dutch law gave married women a number of privileges they did not normally enjoy anywhere else in Europe. Unlike the English goodwife, the Dutch *huysvrouw,* or housewife, could—and often did—run a business, sue on her own behalf, inherit equally with her brothers, and make a will leaving her property to whomever she chose. She might even sue her husband in court—something that would have been literally impossible for an English woman, considered to be legally one with her husband.

Like English traditions, Roman-Dutch law assumed that wives were, in some measure, subordinate to their husbands. But the mutual duties of married couples received greater emphasis than their presumed inequality. To the Dutch and their American-born descendants, marriage was like a business venture in which husbands were the senior partners while wives were prized junior executives.

Of course, systems of law only tell us what a marriage was *supposed* to be—not necessarily what it *was*. Even among the English, female submission was upheld more often in sermons and statutes than in actual practice. In day-to-day reality if not in law and letters, wives in British America were meaningful partners in their marriages. They were not, in any sense, their husbands' equals. But then again, equality had little meaning in the world of Elizabeth Montague Minor Cocke Blaze. What could equality possibly mean when the wealthy planters whose "Great Houses" loomed over the Chesapeake's richer lands could amass thousands of acres while she

Artist John Singleton Copley painted this portrait of Elizabeth Garland Richard (1700–1774), who immigrated to New York City with her parents and married Paul Richard, a merchant who became mayor of New York.

and her family eked out a hardscrabble existence on a small plot of rocky soil? What could equality mean in a world where men and women whose skin was darker were bought and sold like cattle? Equality—at least in the sense we understand it—had no place in her world.

Instead of demanding full legal parity, most wives in the colonies would have rested content with the knowledge that they were, as Puritan minister Samuel Willard put it, the "nearest to equality" among "all the Orders which are unequals." That the wife should submit to her husband's authority was a given. That the obligations between them were also, to a notable degree, mutual, was equally apparent. To an English woman of that time, the belief that her husband was both her ruler and her yokefellow—roles we might see as mutually exclusive—seemed perfectly logical.

Although marriage was based on more than romance, couples who proved compatible often forged bonds of affection, honor, and not least, sexual passion. This was the way that Anne Bradstreet experienced her life as wife and mother. Born in Northampton, England, in 1612, Anne Dudley, a wealthy girl, was schooled by private tutors. When she was just 16 years old, Anne wed Simon Bradstreet. Luckier in the game of survival than the thrice-widowed Elizabeth Montague, Anne Bradstreet found in Simon a lifelong partner. They remained married for 44 years until her death parted them in 1672. Less than two years after her marriage Anne Bradstreet abandoned her comfortable life in England forever. Devout Puritan believers, she and Simon sailed for Massachusetts in 1630. They were among the Bible commonwealth's most prominent inhabitants.

In some respects, Anne Bradstreet's wealth and education set her apart. Even in a setting as rustic as North Andover, the rude hamlet outside Boston she called home after 1644, her high position doubtless meant that her burdens were somewhat lighter than those carried by many humbler goodwives. In other ways, however, Bradstreet's life was typical for a woman of her time.

Like very few women in her day, Anne Bradstreet became a published and widely admired poet. In a place and time where barely half the white women could read and write, Bradstreet was an accomplished woman of letters. Yet she used her writings to affirm the prevailing belief that women were better suited to domestic roles than to public fame. In a series of poems addressed "To Her Husband, Absent on Public Employment," she praised Simon's leadership in the family. He was, she wrote, "my head, my heart, mine eyes, my life, nay more." At the same time, though, she portrayed a marriage that was not a dictatorship but a true partnership. "If ever two were one, then surely we," she wrote in a brief verse dedicated "To My Dear and Loving Husband." "If ever man was loved by wife, then thee." And, as she went on to make clear, the oneness she felt with Simon was physical as well as spiritual. When he was away from her, their lonely bed left her with "chilled limbs." She longed openly for the "sweet contentment" she experienced when they were together.

Of course, such expressions of tenderness do not mean that Anne Bradstreet and others like her were their husbands' equals in any formal sense. Nor, for that matter, was any wife in British America. Married women could not vote. They could not, without special arrangements, own property. They could not stand for office, or serve in the militia, or become ministers. They were not even encouraged to speak in public. They were, in every sense, subordinate to men both within and beyond their families. We should not imagine, however, that this enforced inferiority in law and customs meant

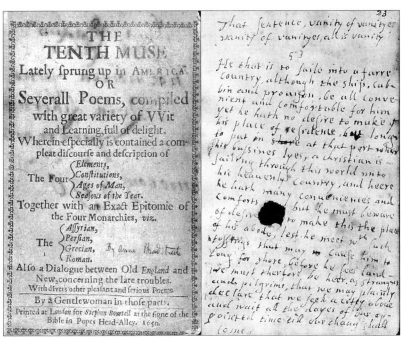

Left, the title page of Anne Bradstreet's The Tenth Muse Lately Sprung up in America, *a collection of poems published in London in 1650. Right, a handwritten page from Bradstreet's* Meditations Divine and Morall. *These meditations, addressed to her son Simon, are reflections on her constant struggle to purify her soul.*

colonial goodwives were, in the words of one common injunction to women, merely "chaste, silent, and obedient."

To be sure, then as now, some marriages flourished while others foundered. A match based on economic and familial concerns might develop into a harmonious partnership. Or the reverse could happen: love could sour, and a marriage might degenerate into a kind of hell on earth from which escape was difficult at best. In New England, where marriage was regarded as a civil contract that the courts could dissolve, divorce was granted when a spouse could prove adultery, unusual cruelty, or desertion. In New York and Pennsylvania, only adultery was considered grounds to terminate a marriage. In the southern colonies the Church of England followed the same rules as it did in the home country; divorce was granted only by a special act of the legislature. Even in Rhode Island and Connecticut, where divorce was available on a relatively liberal basis, few sought to end their marriages. Magistrates in those colonies ruled on an average of only one divorce petition per year throughout the 17th century. For women especially, staying in a troubled marriage often seemed preferable to trying to survive as a single person.

How trying, then, must have been the life of Jane Pattison, who asked the Maryland courts to allow her to separate from her husband in 1736. Though she had been, her neighbors told the magistrates, "a good and dutiful wife," her husband so frequently "beat her with sticks in a Cruel Manner" that they feared for her life. Rachel Davenport, who lived in New Amsterdam in the 1670s, had similar complaints. For "many years," she told the court, "she hath undergone a bitter and wearisome life by Reason of her husband's Inhumane usage." In other cities, the magistrates did what they could to alleviate such suffering.

Though women's complaints against their husbands predominated, wives sometimes took the lead in fomenting marital discord. Joan Miller of Plymouth colony, for example, was charged in 1655 with "beating and reviling her husband, and egging her children to help her." Others, like Goody Lawrence of Essex County, Massachusetts, made words their weapons. In 1681, the magistrates censured her for calling her husband "bald-pated old rogue."

Were women like Lawrence and Miller rebelling against the position of women in their society? Though they rarely discussed their motives, some women in the 17th and 18th centuries appear to have found their roles as wives and mothers literally unbearable. For reasons that are now lost to historians, Salem's Dorothy Talbye was one who did. In 1635 she gave birth to a daughter to whom she gave the ominous name Difficulty, presumably a comment on the labor that produced the child. By 1637, there were signs of serious trouble in Talbye's household. That year the magistrates of the county court found her guilty of "frequent laying hands on her husband to the danger of his life" and sentenced her to the humiliating punishment of being chained to a post in a public square. But the court's rebuke apparently had no effect. Claiming that she had been inspired by the voice of God, Talbye broke her daughter's neck the following year. In December 1638 the authorities of the Bay Colony hanged her on Boston common as a warning to other wayward wives and murderous mothers.

For some women, marriage may indeed have been the kind of earthly paradise Anne Bradstreet described. Others may have been too poor and too careworn even to think much about marital bliss. Still others—women, who, like Dorothy Talbye, were locked in frequent, violent confrontations with their mates and appear to have suffered bouts of deep depression—must have seen marriage as a prison where they were destined to serve time, as the wedding vow said, "till death them did part." It is important to remember, however, that none of these marriages existed in isolation; they were each part of the life of a broader community. Whatever the particular character of her relationship with her husband, every colonial woman would have known that life did not stop at the threshold of her house.

Though she was likely to live in a "nuclear" household—one that included herself, her husband, their offspring, and perhaps a servant or two—the typical goodwife would not have thought of her home as a retreat. For her, the barrier separating family from community was easily breached; women throughout the colonies spent their lives enmeshed in a dense social fabric made up of neighbors, kinfolk, and friends. In happiness and in sadness, in seasons of want and seasons of plenty, colonial women wove the strands of their own lives into the intricate tapestry of their neighborhoods.

At no time would a goodwife have thought her local "community of women" more important than when she prepared to give birth. The onset of "travail" (the early American word for labor and delivery) brought not only pain but genuine fear as well. Although respected midwives often succeeded in even the most complicated deliveries, death in childbirth was still an everyday occurrence. Expressing a sentiment with which any woman would have agreed, Anne Bradstreet wondered in a verse she penned while awaiting the birth of one of her children, "How soon, my Dear, death may my steps attend"? For as many as one woman in five, the answer was very soon indeed.

How comforting, then, that most women did not have to travail alone. Childbirth in the colonial era was not a private ordeal to be suffered through in a distant hospital. Instead, wherever neighbors

The ordeal of childbirth was eased for colonial women by the company and support of their neighbors.

lived near one another, the birth of a baby was an event shared by the whole female community. Particularly in the densely settled villages and towns of New England, the onset of labor pains was the signal for a goodwife to gather "her women" about her. In 1757, when Goody Patten, the wife of a farmer living in Bedford, New Hampshire, "was Delivered Safe of a Daughter . . . after [an] abundance of hard Labor and a great deal of Discouragement," eight neighborhood women were by her side. Men—even fathers-to-be— were kept firmly at bay while local female "experts" (most women would have seen numerous births before they experienced one of their own) served as healers, friends, therapists, and more. Offering refreshments such as the aptly named "groaning cakes" and dispensing traditional herbal remedies, they helped the expectant mother to ease her pain and pass the time between contractions. Offering counsel and speaking from their own experience, they helped to allay her fears.

But would their support have been enough? Only, it seems, in part. Fearing her own death or the death of her infant, a devout woman would also have turned to God in her hour of need. Religion was a palpable presence in the lives of many women in the colonial era—one never so keenly felt as it was during the weary hours of travail.

CHAPTER 4

DAUGHTERS OF EVE, DAUGHTERS OF ZION: WOMEN AND RELIGION

In the beginning was chaos. On that much, the Iroquois and their European neighbors in colonial North America would have agreed. Their respective creation myths—the stories each people told to explain the origins of the world as they knew it—both began with a vast, swirling emptiness. The version of the story favored by the Cayuga (one of the six nations of the Iroquois confederacy) held that "in the beginning there was no world, no land, no creatures of the kind that are around us now." The Bible's book of Genesis, the story that guided the European Christians who sought to bring what they called civilization to Cayuga lands, also looked back to a primordial moment when "the earth was without form, and void, and darkness was upon the face of the waters."

According to both versions of the story, it was from that formless oblivion that the world and all the living things that populated it (humans included) emerged. Humanity, the Iroquois and the Europeans believed, was created by a divine being and sometime thereafter divided into two sexes, male and female. But which sex came first? And what would their ensuing roles be? About such important details, pious Europeans and Iroquois held different views. These differences would be visible not just in their sacred stories, but in their daily lives as well. For religious traditions formed a central

Kateri Tekakwitha, a Mohawk girl converted by Jesuits, was at first persecuted by her people because of her new religion. She later became the first Indian nun and earned the name "Lily of the Mohawks." She died in 1680.

part of the cultures that instructed biological males and females in the ways of acting like men and women.

In the Christian version of the tale, the human race began with a man. According to Genesis, God "formed man of the dust of the ground." Eve followed later, formed from a rib taken from the sleeping Adam. Recognizing their former oneness Adam called her "bone of my bones, flesh of my flesh." She was to be named "woman," he proclaimed, "because she was taken out of Man." (In Old English and in many ancient languages, the word *woman* meant "of man.") From the beginning, then, Christian tradition made woman the second sex—and the weaker sex.

Eve soon proved herself worthy of this designation. Easily tempted, she succumbed to the charms of the wiliest creature in the garden of Eden. "The serpent beguiled me, and I did eat," she confessed, convincing Adam to sin along with her. The price for the transgression was steep. Adam and Eve and after them, all humanity, were driven from the garden forever. But though God punished them both for breaking His laws, Eve was to pay more dearly. "I will greatly multiply thy sorrow," God's voice told her. "In sorrow thou shalt bring forth children." The pain of childbirth, in the Christian view, was a sentence all women suffered for Eve's disobedience. So, too, was their subordination in marriage. Adam and Eve had shared equally in the government of the garden of Eden, but they would do so no more. In the uncharted world beyond the gates she would be his underling. "Thy desire shall be to thy husband," God rebuked her, "and he shall rule over thee."

At the beginning of time, the gods to whom the Iroquois prayed lived in the Sky-World, a kingdom far above the empty earth below. Those gods, male and female, were said to be "like people—like Iroquois." Among them was a woman made restless by the strange cravings that came with pregnancy. Like the Christians' Eve, the Iroquois Sky-Woman had an insatiable desire to satisfy her hunger. At first she sought her husband's guidance, but in time she struck out on her own. Her curiosity brought her to the sacred tree at the center of the Sky-World—a place where, as she soon discovered, the floor of the sky was very thin. Losing her footing, she slipped through a hole at the tree's base and fell headlong "toward the great ocean far below."

Clan Mother, *a contemporary clay sculpture by Tammy Tarbell, a member of the Mohawk tribe. On the statue's stomach are some of the animals that played a role in the creation myth of the Iroquois.*

Sky-Woman came to rest on the back of a great turtle. Without food, she thought she would perish. But the animals of the sea and the air came to her aid. The muskrat—which she named "the Earth-Diver"—fetched from the bottom of the ocean a morsel of soil to place on the turtle's back. From that speck of dirt Sky-Woman created the earth. As she paced in circles following the direction of the sun, the turtle's back expanded into continents for the Sky-Woman to fill with flora and fauna.

Like her Iroquois descendants in North America, this first fallen Sky-Woman farmed the rich earth she created, gathered its fruits, and built a hut upon it to live in. After a time, her pregnancy ran its course and, legend says, she "was delivered of a daughter." The girl and her mother continued to look after their lands till one day, "when the girl had grown to womanhood," a man appeared. He stayed only briefly—just long enough to impregnate Sky-Woman's daughter. When her time to deliver arrived she, like many women during the premodern period, died while giving birth. Her offspring survived: twin boys who would come to rule the earth their mother and grandmother had made. And even in death, Sky-Woman's daughter did not stop nourishing her children. When they buried her in the earth she had helped to cultivate, "three sisters" grew from her grave. The sisters were corn, beans, and squash—staples that would feed the Iroquois and many other eastern woodlands peoples for centuries. One of her twin sons would call himself "Master of Life" or "Great Creator." But this first earthborn woman and her mother were the true providers for the Iroquois nations.

These very different creation myths belong to only two among the countless number of traditions that formed the spiritual base of people's lives in the colonial period. Every native group had its own account of the world's beginnings. For the Pueblo of the Southwest, human life began underneath the earth when a woman named Tsichtinako (Thought Woman) nursed two sisters: Iatikyu, the Mother of the Corn clan, and Nautsiti, the Mother of the Sun clan. The Ottawa, an Algonquian-speaking people living in the northern Great Lakes region, traced their origins to a male figure called the Great Hare and his younger brother.

European beliefs were no more uniform. Though virtually all the whites who settled in colonial North America were Christians

John Fadden, a member of the Mohawk tribe, painted this version of a Mohawk creation story in 1980. The Good Twin struggles with the Evil Twin at the time of creation.

who placed the Bible at the center of their religious universe, they had many different ways of interpreting its meanings. To the Protestants of New England, followers of the teachings of Swiss theologian John Calvin, the devotional practices of the Catholics in New France and the Spanish colonies seemed as alien as those of the Narragansets and Wampanoags who lived among them in Massachusetts and Rhode Island. In turn, the faithful in Virginia and Maryland, who followed the orthodox traditions of the Church of England, considered New England's Puritans to be overzealous reformers. Yet the Quaker radicals who came to the colonies from England in the 1650s and 1660s thought the Puritans too conservative—as did the Baptist rebels who sprang up in their midst. And the few European Jews who migrated to the colonies, concentrating in Dutch New Amsterdam, often met with intolerance from their Christian neighbors. In short, many sects believed that theirs was the true and only way to heaven. But early Americans knew many different roads to salvation.

And yet, despite their many differences, these varied religious traditions held two important things in common. The first was the almost unquestioned loyalty they commanded from their followers. It is hard for us in an era when religion has been separated from much of everyday life to even imagine the level of belief that permeated the premodern world. To be sure, some early Americans were more deeply spiritual than others. But virtually nobody in 17th- or 18th-century America would have considered herself an atheist. Whatever they understood "God" to mean, they would not have questioned the presence of the divine in their world.

Even in the most physical, tangible sense religion was a constant presence. From the stark clapboard spires that capped New England's Congregational meeting houses, to the sturdy brick of Virginia's Anglican churches, to the poles marking the underground kivas in which the Pueblo held sacred rituals, places of worship dotted the landscape. Each and every day, the English villages lining the eastern seaboard would have been alive with the sound of church bells.

Puebloans held their sacred rituals in kivas, structures that were usually underground or in caves.

In less obvious ways, too, religion was a constant backdrop to people's lives. Particularly in the northern colonies, reading from scripture and hearing ministers expound upon its messages were central parts of life. Indeed, editions of the Bible and other religious works were virtually the only printed material available throughout much of the colonial period. For those who could read and those who had God's word read to them, devotional writings, tracts on theology, and tales of wondrous natural events offered needed solace in a fallen world.

The second major thing each of these different traditions held in common was their central importance for women's lives. Figures like the Christian Eve and the Iroquois Sky-Woman offered explanations for the differences between men and women and rules for the ways each gender should act. But religion was much more than a source of prescriptions about the duties of ideal women. It was also a source of emotional support for *real* women. In a world full of

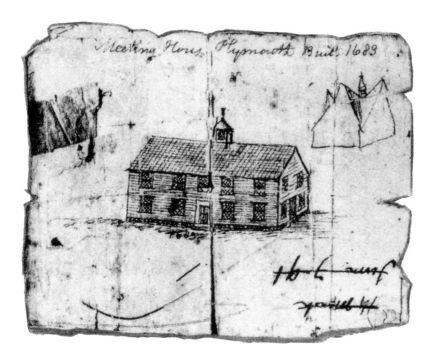

The Second Meetinghouse in Plymouth was built in 1683. Throughout New England, a great part of daily life was centered around the meeting-house.

terrifying uncertainty—the prospect of dying in childbirth and the likelihood of losing a beloved infant, the hardships of living thousands of miles from the land of one's birth or the terrors of invasion by warlike white strangers—religion was a place to turn for help and guidance.

Every part of colonial America had its own rhythms of religious devotion—rhythms that helped women and men make sense of their lives. But nowhere did religion play a greater role than it did in early New England. Almost without exception, the leaders of Massachusetts, Plymouth, Connecticut, New Haven, New Hampshire, and Rhode Island were dissenters from the Church of England. For many of the ordinary people among the first generations of white New Englanders, too, immigration meant more than an opportunity for a better life in economic terms. It was also, more centrally, a chance to live according to what they understood as God's laws—a way of life they found impossible under the Church of England.

Both law and custom enforced the preeminence of Puritan worship (also called Congregationalism or the "New England Way"). Only churches embracing the Puritans' interpretation of Calvin's teachings were permitted. And from the early 1630s until 1662, only the spiritually "elect"—men and women who had personally experienced God's saving grace and felt assured that their salvation had been predestined—could join the Puritan churches. What's more, church membership translated into a voice in civil life; only male church members could become "freemen" and vote in local affairs. Not surprisingly, the communities these freemen-saints designed favored the Congregational way. Biblical mandates became civil laws;

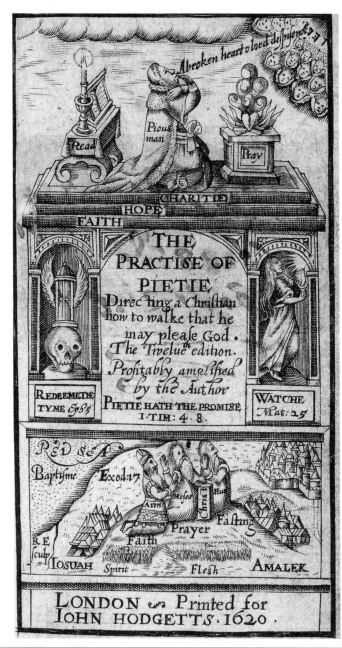

The title page of an early edition of Lewis Bayly's The Practise of Pietie. *Bayly sought to show "a Christian how to walke that he may please God." Such books, called devotional literature, were extremely popular among the Puritans of New England.*

mortal sins like adultery and blasphemy were punishable by death. Sunday, the Christian sabbath, was reserved solely for thoughts of God; no work could be performed. Attending church was mandatory for "saints" (as the "elect" were called) and the unredeemed alike, and the courts regularly punished those who stayed away. Little wonder that, as Boston minister Cotton Mather noted in a 1708 sermon entitled *A Good Evening for the Best of Dayes*, New England enjoyed "the Best Sabbaths of any Countrey under the Cope of Heaven."

No matter whether they enthusiastically supported or dared to question the Puritan mission, all law-abiding New Englanders gathered in their local meetinghouses every Sunday, and often once during the week as well, to hear their preacher expound upon scripture. One perennially popular sermon topic was the nature of women. Between 1668 and 1735, women's lives were the subject of no fewer than *75 printed* treatises. Some of these tracts were funeral sermons that eulogized an especially pious female parishioner; others were more general "how-to" homilies dealing with marriage or mothering. And, to be sure, clerics delivered many more lectures on female piety that were never reproduced in print. Attending carefully to their preachers' instructions, pious goodwives and their mates had many chances to learn about how to divide the work within their families or, as preachers often put it, about the "relative duties" of men and women.

John Cotton, a minister in New Hampshire, offered one such homily on June 19, 1694. On that warm Sunday, John Clark and Elizabeth Woodridge, two of the most prominent inhabitants of the town of Newcastle, were celebrating their wedding. Following a custom that had just taken root in the region, Cotton performed the ceremony himself. (Puritan theologians initially frowned upon such ceremonial uses of the pulpit. Until 1686, only civil officials solemnized weddings in New England.) With his entire congregation gathered for this joyous occasion, Cotton took the opportunity to offer some thoughts about the role of women. The sermon must have hit home with its audience, for it was later printed in Boston and distributed throughout the colonies. We can assume, therefore, that Cotton was saying things that common people—women included—wanted to hear.

John Cotton first published his catechism, Spiritual Milk for Babes, *in 1646. The slim volume was used by generations of Puritans to teach their children religious doctrine. Cotton was the founder of a long line of New England ministers. His grandson was Cotton Mather, and his great-nephew John Cotton was a minister in New Hampshire.*

The text Cotton drew on for his message was Genesis 2:18. The passage described the creation of Eve, foremother of all women in Protestant tradition: "And the Lord God said, It is not good that the man should be alone; I will make him an help meet for him." Precisely what, Cotton pondered in his sermon, constituted a "meet" or fitting companion for a man? What was woman's true nature? Had Eve's daughters living in New England inherited her legacy of temptation and corruption?

On balance, Cotton insisted, they had not. "Women," he told Newcastle's faithful, "are creatures without which there is no comfortable Living for man." In a godly society women were an asset and not, as celibate Catholic priests maintained, a necessary evil. What God had proclaimed at the world's beginning was still true: women "are a necessary Good; such as was not good that man should be without." Woman was not the *same* as man, Cotton was quick to note. Elizabeth Woodridge was not to venture forth into the world but to "keep at home, educating of her children, keeping and improving what is got by the industry of the man." Yet she would not be a mere servant in her husband's house but rather his "most sweet and intimate companion." In God's sight the two were equals of a sort: "joynt Heirs of salvation" in the world to come.

Many New England women took comfort in the spiritual equality of the sexes Cotton and other preachers propounded. Celebrated as "Daughters of Zion," pious matrons took religion very seriously indeed. They attended church without fail and sat rapt while the minister discoursed on the week's text. They read and meditated on the Bible, making their way through the Old and New Testaments at least once each year. They prayed and fasted and experienced God's grace and repented their sins with zeal only the most devout men could have matched.

Pious women were praised by ministers and neighbors alike. If they resembled any Old Testament figure, it was the industrious Bathsheba (the "virtuous woman" described in Proverbs 31:10–31) rather than the perfidious Eve. Where Eve tempted, persuaded, and seduced, Bathsheba planted, prayed, and spun. Her every word testified to a womanly brand of piety: faith tempered with respectful submission. More than one New England minister echoed these verses from Proverbs, exalting the woman who "openeth her mouth with

Anne Pollard, a woman from Massachusetts, was painted holding her Bible in 1721, when she was 100 years old.

wisdom . . . in her tongue is the law of kindness." As the biblical passage suggested, such well-spoken women were indeed more priceless than rubies.

Still, most New Englanders assumed, as minister Samuel Willard noted in a sermon, that woman was "the weaker Vessel." She was ill-suited, Willard and others made clear, for the types of intellectual activity that came naturally to men. One Mistress Hopkins, wife of the governor of Connecticut, was said to have driven herself mad by reading and writing—activities which, John Winthrop noted in his journal, "are proper for men, whose minds are stronger." The sister of Thomas Parker, pastor of Newbury, Massachusetts, received an even harsher judgment of her mental prowess. "Your printing of a book beyond the custom of your sex," her brother told her in a letter in 1650, "doth rankly smell." But even if her mind was thought to be inferior, New England's preachers knew that woman's soul— that part of her which God alone saw—was the equal of any man's.

In fact, New England's "virtuous women" may have been even more devoted to religious practice than their husbands and fathers. At the very least they were more dedicated churchgoers. At first, men and women joined the churches in equal numbers. Within a generation, however, women outnumbered men in many if not most of the churches in Massachusetts and Connecticut. By the mid-1700s, women comprised nearly three-quarters of many congregations. Cotton Mather may not have been exaggerating when he said in an address on the proper *Ornaments for the Daughters of Zion* in 1692 that there were "far more godly women" than men in the world.

The precise reasons for the preponderance of women in Puritan churches are hard to pin down. Some preachers, Mather included, thought that facing death in childbirth brought women closer to God. Many historians now agree. Others suggest that the growing percentage of women in the churches really represents a decline in *male* piety. Whatever the combination of factors bringing them there, women continued to flock toward God's word long after men focused their attentions elsewhere.

"Let your women keep silence in the Churches: for it is not permitted unto them to speak." These were the words of Saint Paul, on women's place in spiritual life, as written in 1 Corinthians 14:34– 35. New England's clergymen regarded these as words to live by. It

Cotton Mather, a prominent Boston minister in the late 17th and early 18th centuries, speculated that women were more devout churchgoers than men because they feared death during childbirth.

was one thing for women to profess virtue, piety, and reverence for God and His ministers. But it was quite another for them to profess their faith loudly, publicly, and persuasively in New England's churches—to *act* like ministers. When women became *too* zealous in their religious practice, they sounded more like daughters of Eve than like daughters of Zion.

Anne Hutchinson was one of the first Puritan women to test the boundaries of female piety in New England. An exceptionally learned and devout supporter of Puritan minister John Cotton, Hutchinson and her husband, William, followed this charismatic preacher from Lincolnshire, England, to Boston, Massachusetts, in 1634.

At first, Hutchinson seemed content within the role the clergy prescribed for laywomen in Massachusetts. As John Cotton later remembered, she had been the ideal "meete helpe" in those early years. Leading small, informal women's prayer groups or "conventicles," and serving as a sometime midwife, Cotton recalled, "shee did much good in our Town."

From Hutchinson's perspective, however, this auxiliary role in religious affairs felt confining. She had serious qualms about the way the colony's churches were being run and sought a larger, more official pulpit from which to air her views. By 1635, she had come to believe, Massachusetts was falling short of its religious goals. Few among the clergy adhered to John Cotton's lofty principles. Where he emphasized the inner workings of divine grace in the souls of true believers, most preachers seemed content with inspiring outwardly pious behavior in their congregations. Like the clergy of the Anglican church, they were more concerned, Hutchinson said, with appearances, or "works," than with redemption, or "faith." It was up to every devout man and woman, Hutchinson believed, to reject the false authority of these inferior clergy: to go over their heads, so to speak, and seek direct communication with God.

Determined to help her neighbors achieve the kind of "immediate revelation" she herself had experienced, Hutchinson began to enlarge her role in the community's religious life. Many in Boston and surrounding towns apparently found her persuasive. By 1636, the prayer sessions in her home had grown to include 60 to 80 men and women—a sizable percentage of the church members in these tiny hamlets. Meeting twice a week to hear Hutchinson preach, these men and women had become a sort of shadow congregation worshiping in their own unconventional style right under the noses of the orthodox ministers.

This state of affairs quickly became intolerable to the colony's leading clergy and magistrates. True, as Hutchinson was fond of reminding them, Saint Paul had declared that "there is neither male nor female: for you are all one in Jesus Christ." But hadn't Paul also proclaimed that "Christ is the head of every man and the man is the woman's head"? That was one lesson Hutchinson had ignored at her peril. It was one thing to hold small meetings in which godly women could reflect upon, and agree with, what their preachers had said the Sunday before. But it was quite another, as John Winthrop later wrote, for Hutchinson to keep "open house for all comers": to become a preacher with disciples who hung on her every word, to reject the teachings of God's rightful ministers. That was nothing short of what the clergy called "antinomianism"—a derisive name meaning "against or opposed to the law" that had been used to describe some of the most hated English heretics.

Salem minister Hugh Peter summed up the male elite's feelings on the matter when he rebuked Hutchinson before the First Church. "You have stept out of your place," Peter said, "you have rather been a Husband than a Wife and a preacher than a Hearer; and a Magistrate than a Subject." She was, others said, a new Eve: a seducer, a trickster, a cunning temptress. Her continued presence in their new world Eden, the elders of Boston's First Church declared, was intolerable. They excommunicated her from the church, and the court banished her from Massachusetts.

That March, Hutchinson, her family, and several of her unrepentant followers were driven out of Boston by order of the Puritan government—sent not to Hell, but to Rhode Island, a colony founded by dissenters from the Puritan establishment and known for permitting a greater range of religious practices than Massachusetts allowed. After William Hutchinson died in 1642, Anne moved with her six youngest children and a small band of believers to a lonely spot in present-day Westchester County, New York. The following year the group was caught in a skirmish with the natives on whose land they were trespassing. Anne Hutchinson and 12 others, including most of her family, were killed; only her youngest daughter survived the attack.

A statue of Anne Hutchinson and one of her daughters. Hutchinson's attempts to claim a public role for herself in the Puritan church led the colony's government to drive her out of Massachusetts.

In the most literal sense, Hutchinson was silenced forever that day in 1643. But her challenge to the Puritan elite and to the confining role they assigned to "virtuous women" lived on. Indeed, Hutchinson was only the first (and possibly the loudest) of a long line of female religious dissenters in New England. She had demonstrated to the clergy that Eve was alive and well and living in Massa-

Anne Hutchinson preaches in her house in Boston, in a romanticized 19th-century depiction. Hutchinson's preaching shocked and outraged the leaders of Massachusetts so much that they excommunicated her.

Unlike the Puritans, the Quakers granted their female members a degree of equality, even allowing women to become lay ministers. Here, a female member speaks at a meeting.

chusetts. Though they would continue to praise pious women who stayed within the boundaries they established, they would remember the lessons Hutchinson taught them as well.

Chief among the dissenting women who followed in Hutchinson's footsteps were those who joined the sect known as the Society of Friends, or the Quakers. One of the more radical groups in the entire spectrum of dissenting English Protestantism, the Quakers granted female believers an extraordinary degree of autonomy and equality. Spiritual rebirth, which Quakers understood as the direct inspiration of Divine Light, came to men and women alike. All those who felt Divine Light working within them could become lay ministers, sharing their transformation with others. Converts of both sexes were encouraged to preach about their religious experiences, and one of the movement's early and most prominent leaders was an English wife and mother, Margaret Fell.

Where the Puritans looked to biblical foremothers like Eve and the submissive Bathsheba, Fell and the Quakers considered such role models irrelevant. Eve's curse and St. Paul's injunctions regarding women's silence applied only to those who had not yet experienced the workings of grace. Reborn in "the Light," Quaker women could pursue more active spiritual roles modeled on the lives of such biblical prophets as Miriam and Hannah. And so they did; the first wave of 59 itinerant Quaker preachers who ventured across the Atlantic between 1656 and 1663 included 26 women.

Mary Dyer was one of them. A follower of Anne Hutchinson in the 1630s, Dyer journeyed to England in 1652 and became a member of the Society of Friends. Convinced that God's Divine Light spoke through her, she returned to New England in 1657 to preach Quaker doctrine. But colonial authorities were unwilling to hear the Quakers' message—especially when preached by a woman—and

This romanticized 1869 painting portrays Mary Dyer on her way to the gallows in 1660. Dyer outraged the leaders of Massachusetts by spreading the Quaker message—in defiance of the colony's laws.

Quaker lay ministers were hounded out of every corner of New England. Dyer was no exception. Banished first from Massachusetts and then from New Haven, she returned to Boston in the summer of 1659. She was again expelled, but defied the court and returned several times more during that summer and fall—even though doing so, Massachusetts law made clear, was inviting the death penalty. On October 19, Dyer and two of her compatriots were sentenced to be hanged. "The will of the Lord be done," she responded to the magistrates who handed down the punishment, "joyfully I go."

At the last minute, Dyer's sentence was commuted to banishment—the one verdict she refused to obey. In May 1660 she returned yet again to Boston, determined to protest statutes outlawing Quaker practice. This final challenge proved to be more than the colony's authorities could bear. Governor John Endicott again ordered her execution—this time to be carried out the very next day. Dyer went willingly to the gallows. "In obedience to the will of the Lord I came," she told the crowd gathered to watch her hanging, "and in His will I abide faithful to the death."

Anne Hutchinson and Mary Dyer were what New England's leaders called "unquiet" women. Pious reflection, rapt attention, and wifely instruction were not enough for them, and they demanded more. Compelled by their faith to take leading roles in religious affairs, they would not rest contented with the models of feminine virtue that the clergy offered. It was a choice for which many women paid dearly.

But Hutchinson and others who followed her lead had more in common as well. Like many other Puritan women who overstepped the boundaries of feminine piety and modesty, they fell under the shadow of witchcraft. Though Hutchinson was never actually tried as a witch, she was clearly suspected. Where Quaker women were concerned, Massachusetts authorities made the links between female preaching, rejecting ministers' teachings, and worshiping the devil even more explicit.

Not all Quaker women preachers were suspected of practicing witchcraft. And not all of New England's accused witches were Quakers. But most of those persecuted for the crime of witchcraft in the British colonies had three things in common with Anne Hutchinson and Mary Dyer: they were female, they were vocal about their dis-

Hannah Callowhill Penn, wife of William Penn, the founder of Pennsylvania. After the Quakers were driven from New England because of their religious beliefs, Pennsylvania offered them a place where they were free to practice their religion in peace.

contents, and they lived in New England. Of the 344 people formally accused of practicing witchcraft during the colonial era, roughly 80 percent were women. (More than half of the small number of men suspected of witchcraft were the male relatives of female "witches.") Virtually all of them came from the colonies of Massachusetts, Connecticut, and New Haven.

Belief in witches had existed in the West since ancient times. But in British North America, witchcraft was largely a failing of Puritan women. It was a crime of overstepping. Those who, like Hutchinson, insisted on acting as if they were more "a Husband than a Wife," more "a preacher than a Hearer" might be accused of carrying themselves more like daughters of Eve than daughters of Zion. Under New England law, the price of such a transgression was life itself.

New England did not possess a monopoly either on religious life or female piety. The North American colonies were home to a wide array of religious traditions, each with unique understandings of women's proper roles. Perhaps nowhere was this plurality of beliefs more dramatic than in the middle colonies, where the sheer diversity of the European settlers meant that no single religious order could easily gain an upper hand. Instead, groups that held widely varying notions of godliness—Presbyterians, members of the Dutch Reformed church, Anglicans, German "Dunkers" (a form of Baptist faith), Jews, and Roman Catholics—lived side by side, if not always in perfect harmony.

It was in this atmosphere of pluralism and relative tolerance that the Quakers sought refuge from the persecution they had encountered in England and in New England. Under the leadership of William Penn, to whom English King Charles II deeded huge tracts of land on the Delaware River in 1681, the Society of Friends began what they called a "Holy Experiment" in the colony they named Pennsylvania. By 1715, more than 23,000 migrants professing many different faiths had followed the Quakers' lead to the Delaware Valley.

The culture that grew up around the Society of Friends in Pennsylvania, Delaware, and parts of western New Jersey was noted for its acceptance of a variety of religious practices, and for its tolerance in another area as well: its endorsement of women's participation in religious life. In the Quaker meetings of the Delaware Valley, a popular Friends' saying—"in souls there is no sex"—took on real force. Although women and men came together for weekly worship, female Quakers also ran their own separate meetings. These so-called "women's meetings" had authority over many issues of church governance. Accused of giving too much authority to women Friends, William Penn explained the role of these separate women's meetings in a pamphlet entitled *Just Measures*, published in 1692:

> "Why should women meet apart? We think for a very good reason. . . . women whose bashfulness will not permit them to say or do much, as to church affairs before men, when by themselves, may exercise their gift of wisdom and understanding, in a direct care of their own sex."

Convening each month as a group, the women of a congregation did indeed look after their own, meting out discipline to female Friends, dispensing charity to the local poor, making decisions about members' marriages, and keeping in touch with other women's meetings in the colonies and in England.

This does not mean that Quakers in the Delaware Valley were feminists in the modern-day sense. A women's meeting sometimes had to seek approval for controversial decisions from the local men's meeting. Quaker men, like their Puritan counterparts, were still recognized as the heads of their households. In social terms, the Quakers may not have considered men and women to be perfect equals. But Quaker women were encouraged to do what Puritan women almost never could: to speak out in religious affairs.

If Quaker women in the middle colonies had more of a voice in spiritual matters than their New England counterparts, white women in the southern colonies were probably even less audible in public worship than were their Puritan sisters to the north. Anglicanism—the state church of England—was the denomination favored in the Chesapeake and lower south. In the 17th century, high death rates and the resulting social chaos made it difficult for churches to take root. But between 1700 and 1750, Anglican parishes, which were supported by taxes and remained largely unchallenged by other sects, grew quickly.

Elite laymen, who could hire and fire their ministers at will, had real power in Anglican churches. But laywomen were expected to follow Saint Paul's instructions and keep silent. Richard Allestree, an English minister who was the leading authority for Virginia's

This pamphlet, An Exhortation to the Inhabitants of the Province of South-Carolina, to Bring their Deeds to the Light of Christ, in their own Consciences, *was written by Sophia Hume and published in 1748.*

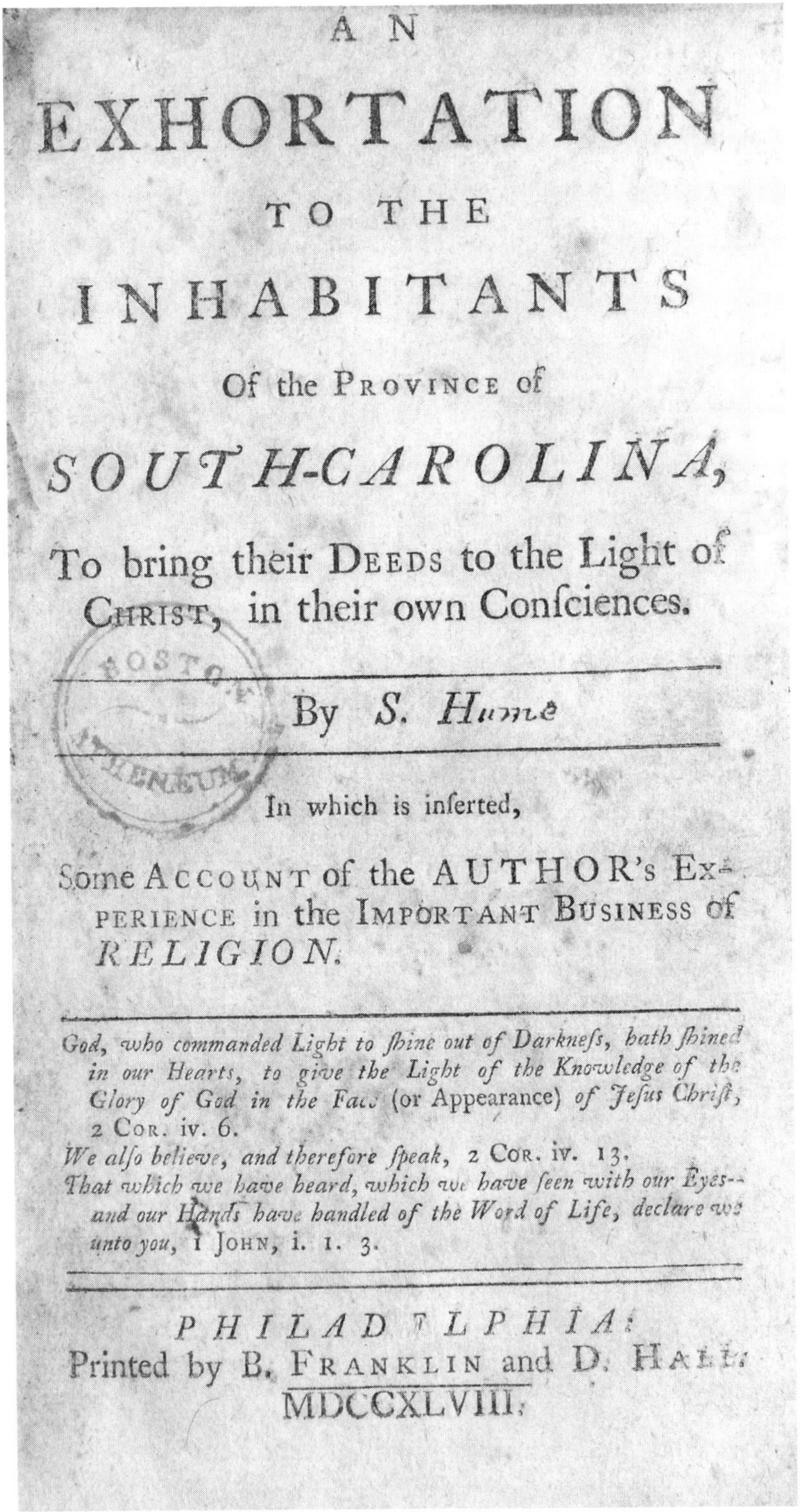

AN EXHORTATION

TO THE

INHABITANTS

Of the PROVINCE of

SOUTH-CAROLINA,

To bring their DEEDS to the Light of CHRIST, in their own Consciences.

By *S. Hume*

In which is inserted,

Some ACCOUNT of the AUTHOR's EXPERIENCE in the IMPORTANT BUSINESS of *RELIGION.*

God, who commanded Light to shine out of Darkness, hath shined in our Hearts, to give the Light of the Knowledge of the Glory of God in the Face (or Appearance) of Jesus Christ, 2 COR. iv. 6.
We also believe, and therefore speak, 2 COR. iv. 13.
That which we have heard, which we have seen with our Eyes, and our Hands have handled of the Word of Life, declare we unto you, 1 JOHN, i. 1. 3.

PHILADELPHIA:
Printed by B. FRANKLIN and D. HALL.
MDCCXLVIII.

Anglicans, explained in a book entitled *The Ladies Calling* that Paul's decree was based on two factors: "the inferiority of the Woman in regard of the creation" and "the presumption that [women] needed instruction." In other words, Allestree said, women should be students and not teachers in religious matters.

Allestree and others recognized, however, that women played important religious roles within their households. What he called women's "native propensions" toward virtue made them important models within their families. And, indeed, many women in the southern colonies were praised for their quiet piety. Occasionally, Anglican women also took more public stances on spiritual matters. Mary Taney, wife of the sheriff of Calvert County, Maryland, was so distressed at the state of religion in that colony in the 1680s that she wrote to the Archbishop of Canterbury, the spiritual leader of the Church of England, to ask for help. The church, she wrote, was in a "sad condition." But she assured the archbishop that her "stray flock" might "prove a nursery of religion and loyalty through the whole Province"—if only they could raise sufficient money to build a church and retain a minister. Taney's plea eventually wound up before the King himself, and he quickly granted her request.

Black women and men brought a very different set of religious beliefs to the southern colonies. Their traditions concerning the supernatural were as diverse as the many African peoples from which they came. There were, however, important common threads; most West Africans believed in more than one God and made the veneration of ancestors an important part of their worship ceremonies. Family and kin were at the very center of African religious life.

Some members of the Moravians, a Protestant denomination, settled in North Carolina in the early part of the 18th century. An evangelical sect, they introduced blacks to Christianity. This illustration from 1757 depicts Moravians baptizing blacks into the church.

Enslaved Africans and their American-born descendants cherished the religious rites they brought with them across the Atlantic, and kept many traditional practices alive under slavery. Slave funerals, for example, were often followed with lively music and dancing—a joyous, exuberant custom common in Africa. Until the 1730s, southern whites made little effort to convert their slaves to Christianity. But in the late 18th century, evangelical sects such as the Methodists and the Baptists appealed to blacks and poor whites alike. Slaves brought many of their own traditions to the Christian services they attended, in large numbers, at the end of the colonial period. Call-and-response hymn singing and joyful shouting are examples of African forms that influenced the style of worship practiced by both whites and blacks in many southern denominations.

Yet another model for women's participation in religion can be seen in the Catholic settlements of North America. In the missions of New France, for example, Catholic women who heard God's call could make religion their vocation. Some who did so were laywomen like Jeanne Mance, who left France for Montréal in 1642 and presided over that city's first hospital. Others were nuns who left the cloistered security of their orders in Europe in hopes of "civilizing" natives in America. Marie Guyart—later known as Marie of the Incarnation—allowed her calling to take her from her secluded, comfortable life in the Ursuline convent in Tours to the distant shores of Lake Québec. Arriving in 1639, she was the first female missionary in New France. During more than 40 years there, she served her God in many ways: as mystic, teacher, and scholar. Her endeavors included founding a school for native children, compiling and publishing a French-Algonquian dictionary, and composing more than 13,000 letters describing life in the French colonies.

From the Ursuline convent to the Puritan "conventicle," from the Algonquian dream quest to the African-influenced styles of worship in the Chesapeake, many different paths connected humans to the divine in early America. And whatever the particular form religious life took in a given locale, women played essential roles. They took solace from the wisdom of preachers and holy texts. And their exemplary lives, in turn, inspired others—male and female alike.

Yet in almost every religious context (the Quakers and some native groups are notable exceptions) the female faithful worshipped within explicit—and often narrow—limits. Nuns were not priests. Daughters of Zion were not ministers of the Word. Female piety did not always add up to female power. As the settlements of the future United States matured, however, many of the conditions that prevailed in 17th-century communities would be called into question. The future of religion and of women's places within it would be chief among them.

Virginia Council Chamber

THE
DISPLAYING
OF SUPPOSED
WITCHCRAFT.

Wherein is affirmed that there are many forts of

Deceivers and Impostors,

AND

Divers perfons under a paffive *Delufion* of
MELANCHOLY and *FANCY.*

But that there is a *Corporeal League* made betwixt the
DEVIL and the WITCH,

Or that he fucks on the *Witches Body*, has *Carnal Copulation*, or
that *Witches* are turned into *Cats*, *Dogs*, raife Tempefts, or
the like, is utterly denied and difproved.

Wherein alfo is handled,

The Exiftence of Angels and Spirits, the truth of Apparitions, the Nature of
Aftral and Sydereal Spirits, the force of Charms, and Philters;
with other abftrufe matters.

By *John Webster*, Practitioner in Phyfick.

*Falfa etenim opiniones Hominum præoccupantes, non folùm furdos, fed & cæcos faciunt, ità ut
videre nequeant, quæ aliis perfpicua apparent.* Galen. lib. 8. de Comp. Med.

LONDON,
Printed by *J. M.* and are to be fold by the Bookfellers in *London*. 1677.

Office

CHAPTER 5

CAPTIVES, REBELS, AND WITCHES: CONFLICT IN THE LATE 17TH CENTURY

By the last quarter of the 17th century, white women and men had been making their homes in various corners of British America for more than 50 years. From New England to the Chesapeake to the West Indies, English settlement was no longer new. All along the eastern seaboard, the desperate urgency of the era of "plantation" had given way to other kinds of problems. At least in older settlements, colonists no longer had to worry about how to subdue a land they considered a wilderness. Instead, they had to grapple what it meant to live there, so far from London (center of their "civilized" universe) on a permanent basis.

No one in the colonies could have helped noticing that there were few founding heroes left to help them make the adjustment. The colonies were no longer filled with men and women who had braved an average of 10 weeks at sea to make the journey from Britain. Even in the disease-ridden Chesapeake, a dip in mortality rates meant that more and more of that region's white colonists had been born not in England but in Virginia or Maryland. In many areas immigration continued steadily and even accelerated. But so, too, did a very different kind of growth: the coming of age of a white population made up not of European migrants but of locally born Anglo Americans.

The title page of John Webster's The Displaying of Supposed Witchcraft, *published in London in 1677. This copy of the book belonged to Virginia's colonial council and was held in the council's chambers.*

When King Charles II retook control of the English government in 1660, he sought to tighten England's control over the diverse colonies and settlements that had sprung up in America.

This shift had potentially dramatic consequences. Would men and women born in these remote provincial outposts remain, in some sense, English? Or would they hold different values and create a different culture from that of their British forebears? Would the towns and villages and plantations in which they lived mature into new Englands? Or were they already becoming something else entirely? These questions went to the heart of the identity crisis that gripped British North America in the late 17th century.

They were also questions much on the minds of European authorities from 1660 onward. That year marked the restoration of the Stuart monarchy in England. Charles II had gone into exile in 1649 when Oliver Cromwell's rebel forces beheaded his father, Charles I, and seized control of the government. But the Cromwellian republic quickly disintegrated, and 1660 found the monarchy back in control. Upon his resumption of power, one of the first issues the younger Charles resolved to tackle was the administration of the colonies overseas. The issue was no longer whether English settlements would flourish in the New World, but how: the political forms they would be permitted to take, the amounts of profit they could be made to generate, and especially, the degree of control London would exercise over them. Beginning with a series of Navigation Acts that Charles II's ministers pushed through Parliament in 1660, the crown would spend the next hundred years trying to shape the loosely knit settlements that dotted North America's Atlantic coast into something more coherent and efficient: a system that might deserve to be labeled an empire.

Doing so would bring about conflicts both within the colonies and without. In North America, the matter would surface as an issue in scattered rebellions throughout the backcountry in the 1670s and 1680s and would finally come to a head a century later when resistance to the crown's efforts to impose tighter controls on exports and revenues would mushroom into a War of Independence.

What would women living in the colonies have made of these grand imperial contests? In one sense the great questions of empire were considered beyond their province. Prevailing views of women's capacities made it unlikely that the average New England goodwife or Chesapeake planter's wife would have much chance to debate the fine points of the economic theory of mercantilism—the belief that

The house of worship, however simple, was a place where the community could gather to pray and to meet. It was a central fixture in many of the new English settlements that arose in America in the 17th century.

the crown should regulate colonial imports and exports. But in other ways, women were very much at the center of the great international conflicts of the day. For all of these immense questions of colonial identity also had immediate local consequences. The collective identity crisis of the late 17th century was felt along the banks of Virginia's James River as well as in the state rooms of Whitehall in London. And women's roles were intimately bound up with this crisis. How would changes in the American landscape—political, economic, ecological, social, and religious changes—reshape their lives? And how would they, in turn, reconfigure the map of colonial America?

In New England, 1675 felt like the beginning of the end. Most of the leaders of the founding generation had since gone on to their rewards in heaven. How could the second, American-born generation live up to the lofty standards of these founding fathers? Every sign suggested that they could not. Anne Hutchinson's early, debilitating challenge had been followed by many others, including the Quaker heretics who had threatened the Puritan establishment in the late 1650s.

Under attack from without, the Puritan experiment also seemed to be eroding from within. By 1662, so few "saints" were seeking admission to the Congregational churches that New England's leaders agreed to soften the rules for membership. A new Half-Way Covenant enacted that year allowed the children of the faithful to become church members without having experienced saving grace, thought to be the key ingredient in humanity's full "covenant" or contract with God.

But even these looser standards seemed too high for such a fallen people to attain. Eleazar Mather, son of founding Boston minister Richard Mather and pastor to the frontier parish of Northampton, Massachusetts, doubted that even the most pious of his generation were equal to the task before them. In a 1671 sermon aptly titled *A Serious Exhortation*, he told his congregation that "the dayes wherein you live are backsliding times, evil dayes, times of great degeneracy," he said. "How hard it is to keep up an House when it's falling down." How hard, indeed? How could they keep their houses in good order when, everywhere they looked, pious New Englanders saw signs of God's dissatisfaction?

As the wife of a Puritan minister, Mary White Rowlandson must have been electrified—and terrified—by such questions. Born in England 1635, she had come to Massachusetts when just a toddler. Thus for all intents and purposes, she belonged to the colony's second generation—the generation of sons and daughters that, as the preachers kept reminding her, was fast sliding into disgrace. Indeed, in the part of New England where Rowlandson dwelled, signs of this decline would have been all too visible. From the bustling seaport of Salem her family had moved north to Wenham, a small farming village founded in 1643. Then, in 1653, the Whites left behind even the minimal comforts of that hamlet when they relocated to a new settlement called Lancaster, an unincorporated village about 10 miles west of Concord comprised of only nine families. Harvard-educated Joseph Rowlandson, the man Mary White married in 1656, was Lancaster's first minister. From the Anglo-American perspective, his tiny parish represented the far western edge of civilization: an exposed frontier at the edge of a howling wilderness. Needless to say, the Rowlandsons thought, Lancaster was hardly the sort of place where a godly life could be easily established.

Just how vulnerable the village was to the forces threatening New England became dramatically apparent to Mary Rowlandson during the winter of 1676. Since the previous June, a bloody war between the English and a confederation of Wampanoags, Nipmucs, and Narragansets (a struggle the Puritans called King Philip's War and the natives knew as Metacom's Rebellion) had raged in villages throughout Massachusetts and Plymouth. It was a conflict which, as Increase Mather, minister of Boston's Second Church, would later write in his *Brief History of the War with the Indians*, was one more sign of God's profound displeasure with the Puritans: another indication that "our sins [were] ripe for so dreadfull a Judgment." And a dreadful judgment it was. Before the conflict ground to a halt in the summer of 1676, both sides suffered devastating losses.

On the morning of February 10, God's "dreadfull judgment" of New England's failings arrived quite literally on the Rowlandsons' doorstep. It was "the dolefullest day that ever mine eyes saw," Mary Rowlandson later remembered, "now is that dreadful Hour come." A war party of Narragansets, whom she called "a company of hell-hounds," laid siege to the village at dawn. Setting fire to barns, overcoming sentries and guard dogs, and killing settlers who got in their way, the party at last arrived at the Rowlandson home, where 37 villagers had taken refuge. In the ensuing melee only one escaped unharmed. Twelve of the English, including several of Rowlandson's relatives, were killed on the spot. Rowlandson and her six-year-old daughter Sarah were shot, and others lay mortally wounded. With her house in flames and her community decimated, Rowlandson, her 3 children, and 20 of their fellow townsfolk were taken captive by the native warriors and driven westward through the winter snow.

During the ensuing 150-mile trek into what Mary Rowlandson called "the vast and desolate Wilderness" (present-day Vermont), she would see everything she knew as civilization recede behind her.

In 1857, Harper's New Monthly Magazine *published this artist's rendering of Mary Rowlandson and her three children, huddled together in a canoe, being taken captive by a band of Narragansetts in 1676.*

Within 10 days of her capture she endured the slow and agonizing death of her wounded daughter, Sarah. Consigning the child's wasted body to an unmarked grave on an unnamed hill, Rowlandson also left her familiar world behind. "All was gone," she wrote, "my Husband gone . . . my Children gone, my Relations and Friends gone, our house and home, and all our comforts within door and without, all was gone, (except my life,) and I knew not but the next moment that might go too." From a world of neat fields, well-maintained fences, and fortified English garrisons, she found herself transported into an exotic land full of people and images and traditions she did not understand.

What did this journey across the gulf separating two such different cultures feel like to this Daughter of Zion? Although Rowlandson remained steadfast in her Puritan faith, the experience of captivity was a deeply unsettling one. Her people had been destined, she thought, to civilize the Indians. But now, she could not help thinking, the Narragansets were making a savage out of her. Rowlandson—against her will—was living the Indians' way: hunting for acorns, greedily gobbling half-cooked horse liver "with the blood about my mouth," dwelling with a Narraganset "master" and "mistress," speaking their language. Eleven weeks and five days passed before Joseph Rowlandson (who was lucky enough to be out of town during the attack) was able to ransom back his wife. After protracted negotiations with her captors, he succeeded in "redeeming" her for the considerable sum of £20. With great fanfare, she was returned to Boston where she rejoined her husband and their two surviving children. She lived the remainder of her days firmly ensconced within the "civilized" English world, first in Massachusetts and later in Connecticut. But memories of her time among the Indians must have haunted her till the day she died in 1711.

However dramatic and difficult Rowlandson's fate, her experience as a captive was not unique. Between the onset of King Philip's War in 1675 and the end of the Seven Years' War (or French and Indian War) in 1763, more than 1,600 whites became Indian prisoners in New England alone. (Of course, the Indians were not the only ones taking prisoners; between the early 16th and late 18th centuries Spanish, French, and English raiding parties murdered, captured, ransomed, and sold countless thousands of Indian captives.)

At least a third of the Anglo-American captives were women; many more were children, of both sexes. The experience of captivity among the natives would hardly have been a welcome one for white men and women who still, appearances to the contrary, considered themselves English. But as the colonial period wore on it was, increasingly, a familiar one.

What is remarkable about Mary Rowlandson's case, then, was not the details of her suffering so much as the fact that she wrote—

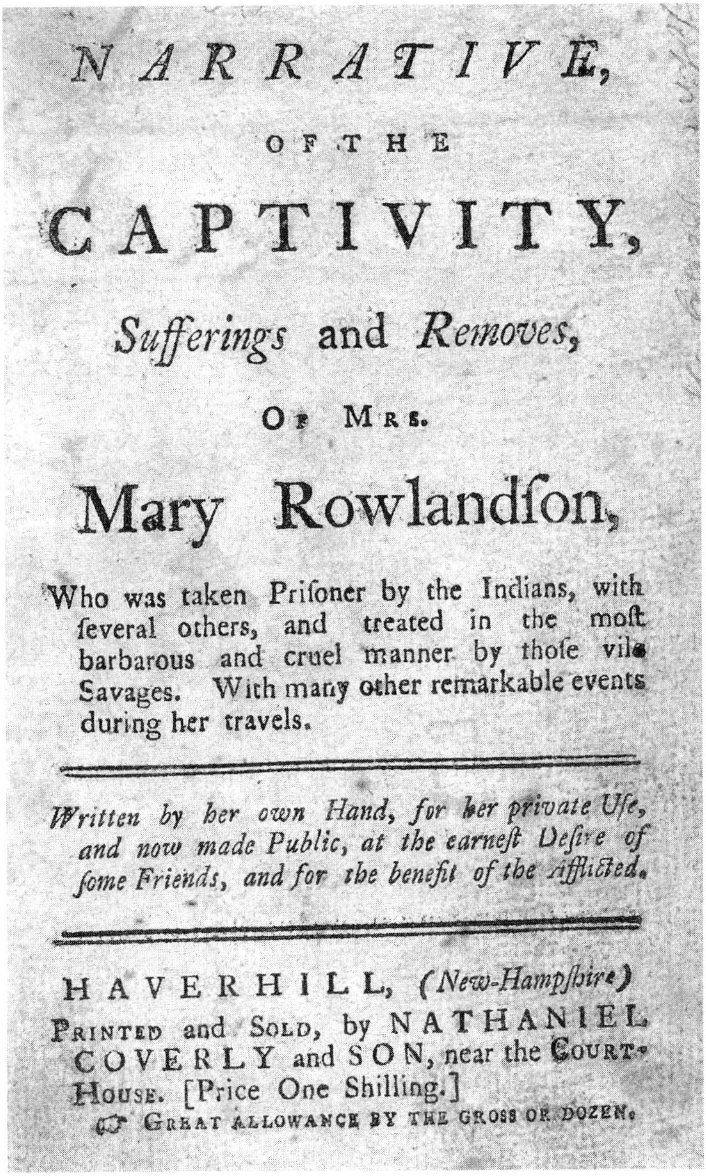

NARRATIVE,

OF THE

CAPTIVITY,

Sufferings and Removes,

OF MRS.

Mary Rowlandson,

Who was taken Prisoner by the Indians, with several others, and treated in the most barbarous and cruel manner by those vile Savages. With many other remarkable events during her travels.

Written by her own Hand, for her private Use, and now made Public, at the earnest Desire of some Friends, and for the benefit of the afflicted.

HAVERHILL, (New-Hampshire) Printed and Sold, by NATHANIEL COVERLY and SON, near the Court-House. [Price One Shilling.]
☞ GREAT ALLOWANCE BY THE GROSS OR DOZEN.

Mary Rowlandson's account of her captivity by the Narragansetts, first published in 1682, was a huge success, going through 22 printings by 1828.

and published—an account of her story. Written in 1677 and first published in 1682, *The True History of the Captivity and Restoration of Mrs. Mary Rowlandson* (also known as *The Sovereignty and Goodness of God*) transformed its author from a private sufferer to a public martyr. The book was an instant success, going through four editions during its first year in print and twenty-two more before 1828. Like Anne Bradstreet before her, Mary Rowlandson became something of a paradox in Puritan society: a woman who publicly and loudly proclaimed her feminine deference and modesty.

In the coming years, there would be many others like her in New England: women whose not-so-silent suffering made them public figures, even heroines, in their communities. Hannah Dustin was one of them. By 1698, Dustin had replaced Rowlandson as the most famous woman in New England. In some ways, she was a more likely heroine. Where Rowlandson had trusted in God, Dustin relied on herself. Captured during a skirmish in King William's War in 1697, Dustin was dragged from the bed in which she had given birth to her eighth child just five days before and forced to march more than 100 miles from her home. Unlike Rowlandson, she did not wait for redemption. Aided by one of her fellow female captives, Dustin picked up a hatchet, murdered 10 of the 12 Indians holding her, and returned to Boston carrying their scalps as proof of her deed. Proclaimed a heroine by the colony's leaders, she broke bread with magistrate Samuel Sewall and heard the eminent divine Cotton Mather memorialize her from his pulpit. She also received a bounty of £25—more than the Narragansets had charged to "redeem" Rowlandson—for the scalps.

Faced with a changing world at the turn of the 18th century, New Englanders were beginning to experiment with different possibilities for women's lives. Amidst the chaos caused by social transformations and Indian wars, some Anglo-American women were deemed worthy of public acclaim—not just for the kind of pious silence St. Paul insisted upon, but also for acts of indisputable, even heroic strength. Women like Rowlandson and Dustin were creating a world in which extraordinary women could become role models for male and female alike. Would such a thing have seemed possible in Anne Hutchinson's day?

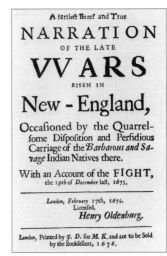

A farther Brief and True
NARRATION
OF THE LATE
VVARS
RISEN IN
New - England,
Occafioned by the Quarrel-
fome Difpofition and Perfidious
Carriage of the *Barbarous and Sa-*
vage Indian Natives there.

With an Account of the **FIGHT**,
the 19th of *December* laft, 1675.

London, February 17th, 1675.
Licenfed,
Henry Oldenburg.

London, Printed by *J. D.* for *M. K.* and are to be Sold
by the Bookfellers, 1 6 7 6.

Tensions between Indians and Anglo-American settlers on the frontier boiled over in the late 17th century. On the left, a band of settlers attacks a Narragansett fort in 1675. The title page of the book above, published in London the same year, attributes the conflict to "the Quarrelsome Disposition and Perfidious Carriage of the Barbarous and Savage Indian Natives" In fact, there was plenty of barbarity on both sides.

Yet for some women, even this expanded sphere of activity still seemed insufficient. There were plenty of female captives who, having been forced to cross the cultural divide separating Puritan from Indian, chose to stay on the other side of it.

Nearly one-third of those taken captive remained among the natives who abducted them. Interestingly, it was not a choice Indian captives would make. As French traveler Hector St. John de Crèvecoeur wrote in 1782 in his *Letters from an American Farmer*, "thousands of Europeans are Indians," but "we have no examples of even one of those Aborigines having from choice become Europeans."

Eunice Williams, daughter of minister John Williams of Deerfield, Massachusetts, was one of the many who did not return. Taken prisoner in a raid on her town during the winter of 1704 at the height of Queen Anne's War, Eunice was only seven years old when she made the long march north to a Kahnawake Mohawk village near Montreal. Her father, her mother, and four of her siblings also numbered among the captives.

But not for long. For the Mohawks knew that the Williamses—an esteemed Puritan family sure to fetch a high ransom—were worth more as diplomatic pawns than as adopted sons and daughters. Negotiations for their release took time to complete. But in late 1707,

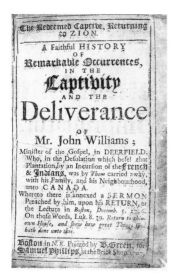

John Williams, along with his wife and five of their children, were taken captive by Mohawks in 1704. After his release was secured in 1707, he published this account of his captivity, The Redeemed Captive Returning to Zion. *His daughter Eunice chose to spend the rest of her life among the Mohawks, much to the amazement of her family.*

some two and a half years after their capture, most of the surviving members of the Williams family (Mrs. Williams had been killed during the trek out of Deerfield) achieved their long-desired aim: a return to "civilization" in Massachusetts. Following in the footsteps of Mary Rowlandson, John Williams quickly published an account of his time among the Kahnawake, a popular treatise that made his sufferings a model all believers could follow. There was only one problem, one obstacle to Williams's happy ending. His precious daughter, Eunice, remained "captivated" in French territory. Now aged nine, she had not been "redeemed" with the rest of his children.

Nor would she ever be. Like many captive women and girls, Eunice came to prefer life among the Kahnawake. Her family reacted with disbelief, unable for many years to accept the reality that she was no longer being held against her will. But when her brother Stephen saw her again decades later, he had to face the truth: Eunice did not *want* to be redeemed. In fact, she was no longer Eunice Williams (English daughter of the most Reverend John), but Marguerite A'ongote Gannenstenhawi (Mohawk wife of a native named François Xavier Arosen, mother of three Kahnawake children, Catherine, Marie, and John). Born Puritan, she had become Catholic. (The Mohawks who captured her had been converted to Catholicism by Jesuit missionaries.) Born to English-speaking parents, she had forgotten the language of her people and adopted the Mohawk tongue. Born a daughter of Zion, she had become something perhaps more powerful, more fulfilling, more meaningful: a Kahnawake mother, a farmer and hunter, a convert to a religion that made saints— even a Virgin queen of heaven—of ordinary women. No, she did not want to go back. No longer Deerfield's Eunice Williams in any meaningful sense, she lived on among her adopted people until the colonies of New England had become the United States. When she died in 1785, she was 95 years old. How distant a memory those first seven Puritan years must have seemed by then!

South of New England, the 1660s and 1670s brought different perils and possibilities for colonial women. The Puritans may have understood the growing pains their settlements faced in religious terms: as a falling away from the lofty goals of the first generation as their settlements aged and expanded. But their countrymen and women in the Chesapeake had no such pretensions about God's favor to begin with. Most English folk in Virginia and Maryland would have agreed that life in their part of the colonial world had started off badly and—with the exception of brief periods during which tobacco prices soared—had only gotten worse. By the 1670s, the crop that fetched three shillings per pound in 1625 was commanding only a tiny fraction of that. Charles II's tightening web of customs law ensured that an ever-increasing percentage of whatever planters could earn at these prices went directly into the pockets of the crown. Leading men who had amassed huge tracts of land were able to enhance their fortunes even at slim profit margins. But ordinary planters in Virginia and Maryland cultivated more and more tobacco (exports doubled between 1670 and 1690) and realized less and less gain from its sale.

In some respects, there was nothing new about this situation. In an era before the modern economic strategy of regulating supply to meet demand was fully understood, raising crops to sell for cash was always a boom and bust business. What was different in the later period was not so much a matter of economics as one of demographics. By the second half of the century, immigrants to the Chesapeake were beginning to live longer. Better provisioned and prepared for the hardships of the region's climate, servants were outliving their indentures and demanding their share of a shrinking economic pie. Enough servants were enduring enough years to become free, marry, and raise families of their own.

They were also living long enough to give birth to *ambitions* of their own—ambitions they could not satisfy so long as they remained poor, landless tenants consigned to farm the immense plantations of an emerging local elite. With land prices high and tobacco profits low, common people found themselves unable to get ahead and seething with resentment. How, they wondered, was the region's new gentry class managing to make a killing in London's markets when common men and women were suffering so? How were planters like royal governor William Berkeley and his wealthy supporters able to grow fat and rich while they—humble men and women, but *English* men and women—worked like beasts of burden just to keep themselves fed? Many couldn't help feeling that Berkeley and his ilk were becoming rich by stealing the products of *their* labor.

Thus, by the 1670s, the Chesapeake was ceasing to be the death trap it had once been only to become a powder keg. And, to a significant extent it was women—ordinary planters' wives—who were behind the shift. After all, it was their increasing fertility that was fueling the growth of the colonies' underclasses. Marrying earlier and giving birth to more children who survived infancy, Anglo-American women in the 1650s and 1660s were becoming the mothers of a restless generation. Surrounded by seemingly endless natural abundance (with so much open land around, why could they not afford to own any?), these young men and women were less willing than their parents had been to do all the work while their supposed "betters" reaped all the rewards. They were angry. They were poor. They were hungry. And they were armed. Most of all, they were waiting: waiting for a chance to get theirs, willing to take it, if need be.

In Virginia, that chance came during the scorching summer of 1675. One July day in rural Stafford County north of the Potomac, several white settlers came upon a small group of Doegs, Susquehannahs, and Piscataways trading in the vicinity. When one of the native traders seized as payment some hogs belonging to Thomas Mathew, he and a group of armed white men pursued the trading party, recaptured the hogs, and killed several Indians. A Doeg war party then killed one of Mathew's servants in retaliation, and the discontent that had long been smoldering among poor white Virginians ignited in earnest. It would take a virtual civil war to put out the flames.

Throughout the summer and fall of 1675, the pattern of Anglo raids and Indian counter-raids escalated. Casualties were heavy on both sides and the white settlers in vulnerable frontier areas looked to their leaders in Jamestown for protection. But Governor Berkeley and other wealthy planters in the Tidewater region wanted to move slowly, preferring to defend their own property rather than to stick their necks out on behalf of the so-called rabble in the backcountry. To those living in Stafford County, Charles City County, and other less settled parts of the colony, the guarded response of Berkeley and his fellow elites amounted to further proof (as if any were needed) that common people didn't count in Virginia. Reaction to the news of Berkeley's hesitation to act was nothing short of mutiny. By the spring of 1676, ragtag vigilante bands sometimes numbering in the

In 1676, settlers on the Virginia frontier, angered over the refusal of the governor and other wealthy landowners to protect them from Indian raids, launched a full-scale armed insurrection that came to be known as Bacon's Rebellion. The settlers were ultimately defeated, but they did manage to capture Jamestown and burn it to the ground.

hundreds had united under two men who supported their cause and opposed the governor: Nathaniel Bacon and Giles Bland. Under their direction, local uprisings became a full-fledged insurrection that would come to be known as Bacon's Rebellion.

From first to last, women were at the center of this escalating crisis. By tradition, they could not serve in the militia, nor could they vote on matters of local policy. In the Chesapeake as in other areas of the Anglo-American world, they had no official status in the public sphere. Nonetheless, in all kinds of unofficial ways, they made significant contributions to the struggle on both sides of the controversy. Indeed, some of the revolt's male leaders held their wives responsible for the initial decision to mount a full-scale insurrection. How could they sit back and wait for help, petitioners on Bacon's side asked the government, while "the cryes of their wives and children" grew ever more "grievous and intolerable?"

To be sure, women in frontier communities had plenty to cry out against. Not only did they suffer disproportionately in the Indian raids; they also suffered humiliating attacks by Berkeley's supporters. A number of women from Charles City County complained against a single loyalist officer, Colonel Edward Hill. One Mrs. Hunt accused him of stealing a precious hogshead of tobacco—the loss of which was certain to make a tough year even more difficult. Servant

Sara Weekes did not get off so easily. Hill held her under guard, accusing her of being an "idle, infamous slutt" known for "robbing, thieving, and whoring."

From Hill's perspective, the attacks on these rebel women were justified by what the armed rebels did to his own wife. While Hill was away fighting the governor's battles to the north and west, Bacon's men had taken over his plantation, gotten drunk on his fine Madeira, and vented their fury on his pregnant wife, Shirley.

Other women were not merely victims caught in the cross fire, but combatants in their own right. Though they rarely took up arms, the support they offered in various ways was an effective weapon of war. Those who sympathized with the rebel faction were instrumental to the cause, providing food and shelter to the troops as Bacon's forces made their way to Jamestown. Mrs. Anthony Haviland, wife of one of Bacon's intimates, took even greater risks, smuggling papers from one end of the colony to the other. Even Colonel Hill admitted grudgingly that Haviland was "an excellent divulger of news."

Charles City matron Sarah Grendon got involved in the insurrection not on her husband's behalf (he was out of the country when the Rebellion broke out) but on her own. Grendon was known to be such a "great encourager and assister in the . . . horrid rebellion" that the governor specifically exempted her from the pardon he later issued to the citizens there.

In the end, forces loyal to the governor triumphed—but not until Bacon's men had seized Jamestown and burned the village to the ground in September 1676. Thus despite their efforts on behalf of the rebellion—efforts which transcended the normal duties of planter's wives—women like Sarah Grendon ultimately found themselves on the losing side. Or did they? As is the case in so many historical questions, the answer is both yes and no. For in the wake of Bacon's Rebellion, the social order in Virginia changed subtly—and the roles of women like Grendon changed along with it. The rebellion had showed the colony's leaders just how volatile the growing ranks of landless, poor freemen and women could be. A shortage of labor to work their abundant lands continued to be a pressing problem for Virginia's elite. But the rebellion drove home the need to find a less costly way of solving that problem than consigning ex-servants to perpetual tenancy in a region where land was plentiful.

Increasingly after 1676, wealthy Virginians came to see the permanent enslavement of black men and women as the best solution to their labor woes. With life expectancies rising, the higher initial price typically commanded by a lifetime slave began to seem worthwhile. With social tensions increasing, wealthy planters were looking for ways to give poor whites a stake in the colony's future. The forced importation of ever greater numbers of Africans answered both of these needs. Denied the possibility of ever becoming free, slaves were not supposed to harbor ambitions for their futures. What's more, this permanent black underclass would, through its very presence, elevate the status of even the poorest whites. Perhaps, elites were willing to gamble, rich and poor Anglo Americans might find a kind of solidarity in the simple fact of their whiteness. In all of these

King Charles II issued this proclamation calling for the arrest of Nathaniel Bacon, the leader of the rebellion in Virginia.

By the King.

A PROCLAMATION

For the Suppressing a Rebellion lately raised within the

Plantation of Virginia.

CHARLES R.

Hereas Nathaniel Bacon the Younger, of the Plantation of Virginia, and others his Adherents and Complices (being Persons of mean and desperate Fortunes) have lately in a Traiterous and Rebellious manner levyed War within the said Plantation, against the Kings most Excellent Majesty, and more particularly being Assembled in a Warlike manner to the number of about Five Hundred Persons, did in the Moneth of June last past, Invir on t Besiege the Governor and Assembly of the said Plantation (then met together about the Publique affairs of the same Plantation) and did by Menaces and Threats of present Death compel the said Governor and Assembly to pass divers preten ded Acts : To the end therefore that the said Nathaniel Bacon and his Complices may suffer such punishment as for their Treason and Rebellion they have justly deser ved; His Majesty doth (by this His Royal Proclamation) Publish and Declare, That the said Nathaniel Bacon, and all and every such Persons and Person, being His Majesties Subjects within the said Plantation, as have taken Arms under, willingly joyned with, or assisted, or shall hereafter take Arms under, willingly joyn with, or assist the said Nathaniel Bacon, in raising or carrying on the War (by him as aforesaid levyed) are and shall be guilty of the crime of High Treason. And His Majesty doth her eby strictly Charge and Command all His Loving Subjects, That they do use their utmost endeavour to Apprehend and Secure the Persons of the said Nathaniel Bacon, and of all and every the said Complices, in order to the bringing of them to their Legal Tryal. And for the better encouragement of His Majesties said Loving Subiects to Apprehend and bring to Justice the respects, Virginia's governor noted in 1683, "Blacks can make [tobacco] cheaper than Whites."

The sudden, dramatic growth of the enslaved population indicates that many elite Anglo Americans agreed with the governor. From a population of roughly 500 at mid-century, the enslaved labor force in Virginia and elsewhere in the colonial south mushroomed. The 11 years between 1698 and 1709 alone saw the importation of twenty times that many slaves to Virginia. By 1775 there were more than 250,000 blacks in the Chesapeake—nearly half the region's total population. Further to the south, the proportion of black inhabitants was even higher. From Maryland to South Carolina, African-born slaves and their American-born descendants had all but replaced white servants by the second quarter of the 18th century.

How did this shift affect women's lives? The answers depended upon the color of a woman's skin. For the planter wife, the turn toward slavery likely meant a life of increased ease. No longer would she find herself consigned to the very bottom of Virginia's social order, forced to labor in the fields like the meanest English peasant wife. No longer would she have to bow and scrape to the gentry in Jamestown. Now, as a white woman, she was in a sense one of them.

For the thousands of black women who were brought to the Chesapeake in chains in the years after Bacon's Rebellion, the answers would be altogether different. Captured from such diverse West African regions as modern-day Nigeria, Angola, and Sierra Leone, they lacked even a common language in which to share their sorrows. In time, however, their descendants would form a distinct African-American culture: a culture enduring enough to sustain its members through the hardships of slavery and strong enough to encourage many to claim their freedom whenever a chance presented itself. And in their world, no less than in the world of the white plantation owners, women would often lead the way.

As workers in the fields and as breeders of human property, black women were forced to serve the needs of their owners. Increasingly, they would also find themselves serving within the homes of elite planters. Virginia planter William Byrd II, for example, employed a number of female slaves inside the "great house" he called Westover, including a cook named Moll, a baby nurse called Anaka, and Mistress Byrd's personal maid, Prue. The labor such women performed was no less arduous than fieldwork. Their workday began at sunrise and often lasted late into the night. Indeed, it was their labor that enabled plantation owners to live in the genteel style upon which visitors to the southern colonies often remarked.

Within the plantation household and in the fields of the southern colonies, black women contributed to the comfort and wealth of the white ruling class. But within their own quarters, they worked to sustain their kin under the harshest possible conditions. In doing so, black women kept alive diverse African traditions while forging new, uniquely African-American ones.

In many African cultures, the bond between mother and children was considered especially strong. This tradition took on new importance under slavery. Male slaves were often sold away from their families, but many masters proved reluctant to separate young children from their mothers. Slave women typically lived with their sons and daughters until the children were at least 10 years old. Therefore, mothers, more often than fathers, taught their children how to survive the slave system. Black women were also central to the dense networks of kin that grew up among slave family members who had been sold to neighboring plantations. The sense of connection provided by these wider circles of aunts, uncles, ex-spouses, cousins, and step-siblings helped slaves to compensate for the vulnerability of their individual households.

The growing pains experienced by the British colonies in North America at the end of the 17th century had different meanings for different women. Some, like Lancaster's Mary Rowlandson, might find in the upheaval new possibilities for airing their views. Others, like Charles City's Sarah Grendon, might find new calls to action. And still others, like William Byrd's enslaved maid Prue, undoubtedly found new hardships and the momentous task of forging a new culture in this changing world.

In Salem, Massachusetts, women confronted all of those perils and possibilities at the end of the 17th century. For it was there, in 1692, that the most extensive witch-hunts ever seen in the colonies took place. By that time witchcraft had a long history in British North America. Beginning in the 1630s, prosecutions of women suspected of practicing witchcraft continued sporadically throughout the 17th century. In Salem, as in other locations, women comprised

Mary Willing Byrd, the wife of Virginia planter William Byrd III. In the 18th century, wealthy landowners in the South used an increasing number of slaves to work on their growing plantations and inside their lavish mansions.

the vast majority of those accused—as well as a significant proportion of the accusers and some of the most vocal "victims." Thus the crisis at Salem belonged, in part, to a very old pattern, a Puritan pattern in which the Devil almost always seemed to appear in the shape of a woman.

But there were different things about Salem, too. For one thing, there appeared in Salem new sorts of "devils" to fight against: the rapid growth of the population, the spread of commerce, the feuding of neighbor against neighbor. And there was also, at Salem, an entirely new scale to the prosecutions. Between the day the first charges were leveled in January 1692 and the end of the trials early the following October, approximately 156 people in 24 towns had been accused. Nineteen of them—fourteen women and five men—had been

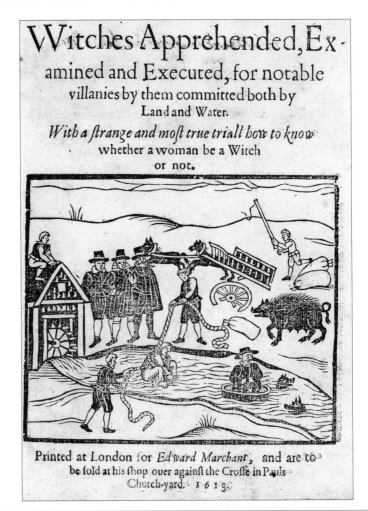

This book, printed in London in 1613, offered English readers accounts of some of the "notable villanies" committed by witches, along with various "trialls" designed to determine whether a woman was a witch.

hanged; one man had been pressed to death with heavy stones. Just what had plunged Salem and many nearby villages into such a panic?

If we could interview someone from late-17th-century Salem Village, the part of town that was home to most of the accusers, she would probably say that the story began one icy January morning in the kitchen of the Reverend Samuel Parris, minister of Salem Village. There, several girls and young women, including Parris's daughter, Betty (aged nine), and his niece, Abigail Williams (aged eleven), began an innocent game of divining: looking to the occult for signs about who their husbands might be. Perhaps such questions were themselves a sign of the times—an indication that in the growing towns of New England, the identity of one's future mate was no longer as predictable as it once had been. Whatever the reason for their curiosity, excitement soon gave way to fear as the girls experienced what they described to local ministers as a feeling of being "bitten and pinched by invisible agents . . . taken dumb, their mouths stopped, their throats choked, their limbs wracked and tormented." News of their "cruel Sufferings" spread through the village, and many who heard descriptions of their "fits" knew immediately what the cause must be: witchcraft.

As the winter wore on, Betty Parris, Abigail Williams, and several of their friends displayed their "afflictions"—real or pretended—for ever larger audiences. By June, young women living as far away as Boston, where some of the accused were jailed, had experienced similar symptoms. And plenty gathered to see them perform.

Perhaps, like Mary Rowlandson, these young girls were eager to claim a larger space for women's voices in a changing world. Perhaps they truly *were* suffering—not from what we today would understand as witchcraft, but from some other mental or physical illnesses. To their audiences, however, our questions about the "real" reasons for their celebrated fits were very much beside the point. The explanation was readily at hand in the shape of three local women whom the girls accused of tormenting them.

Only the first of the three, Sarah Good, fits traditional stereotypes of the witch. Pregnant, poor, and homeless, she was known in Salem Village as an outspoken malcontent—a personality type that often turned women into witches in their neighbors' eyes. The second woman accused was Sarah Osborne, a former resident of

Samuel Sewall, one of the judges who presided over the witchcraft trials at Salem in 1692. In January 1697, during a Fast Day set aside for Boston's inhabitants to meditate upon the deaths of 20 innocent men and women accused of witchcraft in 1692, Sewall offered a public apology, proclaiming his "Blame and Shame" and "Asking pardon of Men" for his role in the trials.

Watertown who had moved to the village in 1667. Like many suspected witches, Osborne had defied local norms where inheritance was concerned. With the help of her second husband, she contrived to retain control of lands and moneys that she should have passed on to her children. Accused on February 29, 1692, she died in jail early that May.

The third among the initial suspects proved to be in many ways the most important. Where the others denied they were witches, she confessed to the crimes of which she was accused and thus helped fuel the mounting spiral of accusations, counter-accusations, confessions, and hangings. Where Good and Osborne had been locals, she was in every sense an outsider. She had only one name, Tituba. Much about her remains shrouded in myth. Sometimes she is described as a black slave, while other accounts call her an Indian servant. Her husband, John Indian, was almost certainly a local Native American. But she was a stranger who had come to Salem from the sugar island of Barbados—a symbol of the thickening web of trade between Britain, Africa, the islands, and the mainland that supplied the southern colonies with slaves, New England with cash, and England with sugar, rum, and finished goods.

Whatever the tangled path that brought Tituba to Salem, her presence there had far-reaching consequences. Her stories of witches' sabbaths, spectral yellow birds, and flights through the sky on a

The warrant for the arrest of Ann Pudeator, one of the women accused of witchcraft in Salem, signed by magistrate John Hathorne. Hathorne's illustrious descendant, Nathaniel Hawthorne, struggled to come to terms with his ancestor's deeds and wrote highly negative portrayals of the Puritans.

broom entranced her judges and provided motifs others would later echo. After Good, Osborne, and Tituba told their stories in March, accusations and trials came thick and fast. By the end of April, Essex County's jails were packed with suspects—one of whom, young Dorcas Good, was no more than four years old.

On June 10, the first hanging was carried out as Bridget Oliver Bishop—a woman long known for her belligerence toward her husband—was led to the gallows. By the end of the summer, so many more would follow in her footsteps that the place of her execution would earn the name "Witch Hill."

To a one, each of the women who met her end on that hill maintained her innocence. Among the most eloquent was Sarah Good, hanged on the afternoon of July 19, 1692. As she stood on the gallows, the Reverend Nicholas Noyes urged her to confess her sins before the large crowd assembled to hear her last words. But Good, known all her life as a "turbulent spirit," did not go quietly. "You are a liar," she spat in Noyes's face. "I am no more a Witch than you are a Wizard, and if you take away my Life, God will give you blood to drink."

The trials at Salem were testimony both to the enlarged possibilities of Anglo-American women's lives in the late 17th century, and to the limits within which women continued to live and think, write and speak. As afflicted girls, as Indian captives, as supporters of a male-led rebellion, some women experienced new power in the last quarter of the first century of the British colonial experience. But Salem reminds us that in the late 17th century women could only be accusers, or victims, or "witches"; they could not be preachers or judges. The new century would bring significant changes to their everyday lives. Yet as the colonial world expanded, the formal channels of education and public power remained beyond their reach. This central fact, made so dramatically manifest in 1692, would remain unaltered for many years to come.

The punishment for witchcraft was hanging. In Salem, more than 100 people were tried as witches; 20 people and 2 dogs were put to death.

CHAPTER 6

AWAKENING AND DIVERGING: 18TH-CENTURY TRANSFORMATIONS

The year was 1734, a time of relative tranquillity in the British settlements of North America. Queen Anne's War had ended more than two decades before and the next round in the imperial contest had not yet begun. The non-Indian population of the colonies was growing steadily: already at 210,000 in 1690, it had reached 400,000 in 1720 and was continuing to climb. By 1776 it would top 2.5 million. Part of the increase was natural, as large families had become the rule everywhere in the colonies. In addition, each year saw waves of new immigrants arrive as the ongoing exodus from England was supplemented by a flood of refugees from other European lands (thousands of Scots-Irish, Swiss, Germans, and French along with a scattering of Welsh, Swedes, and Dutch) and by increasing numbers of Africans forced to migrate against their will.

But even this influx failed to put a damper on the soaring colonial economy. With exports fetching high prices and land remaining cheap and plentiful, most Anglo Americans were able to do what their counterparts in Europe could only dream of: to live on their own family farms. Descended from a world of tenants (in England, a tiny minority of wealthy families owned over three-quarters of the tillable acreage), they had created a world of independent yeomen beholden to none.

A fanciful 18th-century seat cover. As the colonies matured, the lucky few were able to surround themselves with such household luxuries.

Jonathan Edwards was the pastor of the Massachusetts village of Northampton in 1734 when some of the town's young people began to experience strange physical symptoms. These symptoms were signs not of the presence of the Devil but of the beginning of a religious renewal that swept across parts of British America.

Or so it seemed on the surface. But though the British colonies in 1734 may have looked like peaceable, prosperous kingdoms, the elders in the western Massachusetts village of Northampton were worried. For in their sleepy town, groups of young people had begun to display strange, inexplicable symptoms. The town's Yale-educated pastor, Jonathan Edwards, noted their "great terrors" and "sudden distresses," signs of what he called a "struggle and tumult" that bordered on "despair." His parishioner Abigail Hutchinson had manifested many of these "distempers." Only 19 years old, she was gripped by what Edwards described as "exceeding terror . . . her very flesh trembled" before his eyes. Other young women spoke of frightening visions, including an apparition of a gaping, "dreadful furnace" only they could see.

Just what had driven the youth of Northampton into such a state? Some among the faithful could not help wondering whether they were witnessing a resurgence of the tensions that had plagued Salem more than 40 years earlier. Once again, they pointed out, young women were wailing and weeping in public while powerful men doted on their every word. Once again there were rumors that the Devil was afoot. Many signs hinted that 1734 could turn into a repeat performance of 1692.

But, in the end, folks in Northampton (and in towns all along the eastern seaboard where similar disturbances had arisen) advanced another explanation for the turmoil. Instead of turning toward the Devil, people came to believe these ecstatic young women were embracing the Lord. Their "fits" were not signs of demonic possession but of religious conversion. Girls like Northampton's Abigail Hutchinson were not latter-day versions of Salem's loudest accuser, Abigail Williams; they were the vanguard of a movement of religious renewal that eventually overtook so many parts of British America that it earned the name "Great Awakening."

The revivals in Northampton were among the first sparks in what quickly became a fire storm of religious enthusiasm. The ensuing Great Awakening was not a single event but rather a series of "mini-awakenings" that took place from the 1730s through the 1760s and stretched from Britain to Maine to Georgia. Rejecting what they saw as the tendency of so-called "Old Light" preachers to over-intellectualize doctrine, "converted" or "New Light" ministers spoke

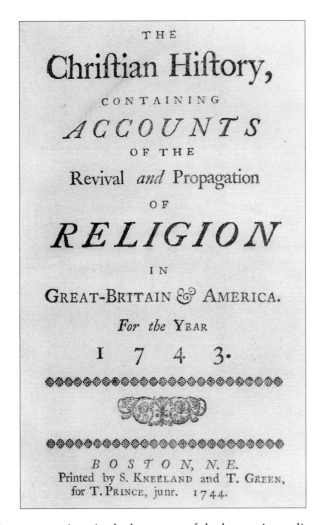

THE
Chriſtian Hiſtory,

CONTAINING

ACCOUNTS

OF THE

Revival *and* Propagation

OF

RELIGION

IN

GREAT-BRITAIN & AMERICA.

For the YEAR

1 7 4 3.

B O S T O N, N. E.
Printed by S. KNEELAND and T. GREEN,
for T. PRINCE, junr. 1744.

An evangelical tract published in Boston during the Great Awakening.

to their congregations in the language of the heart. Appealing to passion as well as to reason, their oratory proved to be a powerful draw to masses of common men and women who found themselves eager, as Edwards later wrote, "to drink in the words of the minister."

This sudden desire to "drink in" God's word was not confined to New England. Signs of a new religious foment surfaced somewhat earlier in the middle colonies, where the growing ethnic diversity of the population had produced an expansive array of Christian traditions. By the early 18th century, Pennsylvania, New Jersey, New York, and Delaware were home to an almost dizzying variety of denominations, including Presbyterians, Lutherans, Mennonites, Huguenots, Quakers, Baptists, Anglicans, and several smaller utopian sects.

The mix of peoples and beliefs proved to be a volatile one. In Presbyterian congregations throughout New Jersey and Pennsylvania, Scots-Irish immigrants and their descendants embraced the fiery rhetoric of evangelical or "New Sides" ministers. By the 1730s, many laymen and women were flocking to hear the sermons of revivalist preachers such as George Whitefield, a young, itinerant English minister (that is, one who was not based in one place but traveled from town to town to preach); Dutch Reformed leader Theodorus Frelinghuysen; and the Scottish-born William Tennent and his sons.

The frenzy that greeted the arrival of young English minister George Whitefield in 1739 showed how eager common men and women were to hear God's word as interpreted by the revivalists.

English itinerant preacher George Whitefield was one of the most popular preachers of the Great Awakening. On April 10, 1740, the Pennsylvania Gazette *devoted its front page to a letter from Whitefield.*

APRIL 10. 1740.

NUMB. 591.

The Pennsylvania GAZETTE.

Containing the freshest Advices Foreign and Domestick.

A Letter from the Rev. Mr. WHITEFIELD, at Georgia, to a Friend in London, wherein he vindicates his Asserting, That Archbishop Tillotson knew no more of Christianity than Mahomet.

Savannah, January 18. 1739,40.

My Dear Friend,

THO' that Saying of the Psalmist, *Thou shalt answer for me, O Lord my God*, has generally been a Rule for my Conduct, in respect to my Adversaries; yet when the Glory of God and the Welfare of his People are concern'd, I think it my Duty to maintain whatever I have asserted in any of my Discourses, either publick or private.—My affirming *That Archbishop* Tillotson *knew no more of Christianity than* Mahomet, has been look'd upon as one of the most unjustifiable Expressions that ever proceeded out of my Mouth: For this I am not only look'd upon as a greater Monster than ever by my Enemies, but also have been secretly despised and censured by some, who, otherwise, were my Friends. Indeed, I dare not say this Expression came originally from me: No; my dear and honoured Friend Mr. *John Wesly*, if I mistake not, first spoke it in a private Society, when he was expounding Part of St. *Paul's* Epistle to the *Romans*, and proving the Doctrine of Justification in the Sight of God, by Faith alone, in Contradistinction to good Works. It is in this particular (not to mention others) that I have and do now join Issue with my honour'd Friend, and upon the maturest Deliberation, say again what I have often said before, *That Archbishop* Tillotson *knew no more about true Christianity than* Mahomet. — Whatever high Opinion others might have of that great Man and his Works, I must confess he was never a Favourite of mine. My Sermon on *the Eternity of Hell Torments* was directly level'd against a Discourse of his on that Subject, before I left the University: And since I came from thence, my Dislike of him has been much encreas'd, because I have observ'd all natural Men generally speak well of Archbishop *Tillotson's* Works. — And if we may judge of Men's Writings as well as themselves, by our Lord's Rule, we cannot but pronounce a Woe against those Books which natural Men generally speak well of. Did he teach the Truth as it is in Jesus, Thousands, who now admire, would throw

aside his Discourses as waste Paper. — But I would not lay all the Stress of my Objections here — Out of his own Writings will I prove my Assertion. — Any spiritual Man that reads them, may easily see that the Archbishop knew of no other than a bare historical Faith: And as to the Method of our Acceptance with God through Jesus Christ, and our Justification by Faith alone (which is the Doctrine of the Scripture and the Church of *England*) he certainly was as ignorant thereof as *Mahomet* himself. — It would be endless to produce all the Passages out of his Sermons, that prove this; I shall only refer every impartial Reader to *Vol. 2d. Serm. 52d. 53d. 54th. 55th. 56th.* The Title of which runs thus —" On the Nature of Regeneration, " and its Necessity, in order to our Justification and " Salvation." So that according to this Title, His Grace intended to prove, that we must first be regenerated and sanctified, and then on Account of that Regeneration or Sanctification, that God will justify, *i. e.* acquit, accept and reward us. — That I do not wrong the Archbishop, is plain from this Passage in *Sermon 52d. page 325, Folio.* " All that the Gospel requires as " necessary to these Purposes (*i.e.* to Man's Justification " and Salvation) is that we perform the Conditions of " the Gospel, that so we may be capable of being made " Partakers of the Blessings of it." And at the End of *Sermon 56*, which is the last on that Subject, and as the Summary of what he had before been delivering, He writes thus —. " You see then what it is that must " recommend us to the Favour of God. The real " *Renovation* of our Hearts and Lives after the Image " of him that created us, before ever we can hope to be " restored to the Grace and Favour of God, or to be " capable of the Reward of eternal Life: And what " could God have done more reasonable than to make " those very Things the Terms of our Salvation, " which are the necessary *Causes* and Means of it? " How could he have dealt more mercifully and " kindly with us, than to appoint that to be a Condition of our Happiness which is the only Qualification " that can make us capable of it?" Had St. *Paul* been alive and read this Passage, I am perswaded he would have pronounced an ANATHEMA against the Writer of it, as he did against the *judaizing Teachers* in the Church of *Galatia*. — For what can be more contradictory to the Gospel of Jesus Christ: Here is not a Word mention'd about the all-sufficient, perfect and everlasting

For Hannah Harkum Hodge, the daughter of a Calvinist minister in Philadelphia, hearing Whitefield preach figured as the central moment in her long life. When she died in 1805 at the age of 84, her obituary described a devotion that led her to follow the preacher "on foot" from Philadelphia "to Chester, to Abingdon, to Neshaminy, and . . . even to New-Brunswick, in New-Jersey, the distance of sixty miles." Hannah later became a leader in her community's religious life, and her home was known as "a place for prayer and religious improvement."

Whitefield and other revivalists showed a unique ability to entice men back into the fold. But although record numbers of male converts returned to the churches during the 1730s and 1740s, female voices accounted for a majority of those professing an "awakened" or reborn faith. And, for the first time during the revivals of the Great Awakening, women delivered their testimony not in private conferences with their ministers, but openly, loudly, and publicly.

Sarah Pierpont Edwards was another of the tens of thousands of young women swept up in the religious fervor of the mid-18th century. Born in New Haven in 1710 to a family of prominent Puritan ministers, young Sarah was widely known for her devotion to God. When she was just 13, she attracted the attention of Jonathan Edwards, who was then studying for the ministry at Yale. Writing in his private journal, Edwards praised Sarah's "strange sweetness" and "singular purity." Perhaps he knew that day that he had found his "meete helpe"; four years later the two were married.

If any woman could have felt certain that divine grace dwelled within her, surely it was Sarah Pierpont Edwards. But, perhaps prompted by her husband's hellfire and brimstone preaching, she began in the late 1730s to fret about the state of her soul. Over the next several years, she unflinchingly contemplated her own sinfulness, striving, as she put it, to be "swallowed up, in the light and joy of the love of God." So moved was her husband by Sarah's relentless probing of her innermost failings that he asked her to write a detailed account of the experience—a narrative which even today brings to life the momentousness of what some women experienced during the Great Awakening.

In January 1743, Sarah Edwards reached the depths of despair. "I felt very uneasy and unhappy," she wrote in her "exact state-

Sarah Pierpont Edwards was encouraged by her husband, the minister Jonathan Edwards, to record her innermost feelings as she struggled with her soul.

ment" of her conversion experience, "at my being so low in grace." Shaken from her earlier sense of security in God's love, she began to feel "a deep abasement of soul . . . a sense of my own unworthiness." Throughout the month, her spirits alternated between elation and terror as she tried to bring herself closer to God.

The break in this cycle of repentance, assurance, and renewed doubts came during a sermon preached by a local itinerant, Samuel Buell. Buell's lecture on January 27 convinced Sarah Edwards that "God was present in the congregation." She swooned during the homily. When she returned home that evening the talk was again of God. Reverend Buell and several other area ministers had gathered at the Edwards' house to chat about "Divine goodness." As the pious group talked and sang psalms, Sarah felt so moved that she had to fight off the urge to dance for joy.

Her euphoria reached an ecstatic peak during the night of January 28. "That night," she remembered, "was the sweetest night I ever had in my life." Staying awake almost till dawn, Sarah experienced perfect union with God—"a constant flowing and reflowing of heavenly and divine love." So intense was this feeling that it seemed she had escaped her body. A single minute of this "heavenly elysium," she wrote, "was worth more than all the outward comfort and pleasure, which I had enjoyed in my whole life."

The next morning she could not contain her joy. When one of her husband's friends called at the house she greeted him saying, "I have dwelt on high in the heavenly mansions . . . my soul has been lost in God." Yearning to tell all who would listen about the experience, Sarah described the previous night's raptures for "about a quarter of an hour." Secure at last in her salvation, Sarah Edwards continued to be an inspiration to her husband and their nine surviving children until her death from dysentery in 1758.

Although Edwards's description of being "swallowed up in God" is particularly eloquent and detailed, many more humble female believers described similar feelings. Anxiety and doubt. Assurance and rapture. And, above all, an intense desire to *testify* to their experience. The initial probing was always unsettling. But after what one young convert called this "dreadful distress of soul" came sweet relief. For Mary Shumway of Sturbridge, Massachusetts, the feeling was one of almost instantaneous release. "My fears vanished as a

SINNERS

In the Hands of an

Angry GOD.

A SERMON

Preached at *Enfield, July* 8th 1 7 4 1.

At a Time of great Awakenings ; and attended with
remarkable Impreffions on many of the Hearers.

By *Jonathan Edwards,* A. M.

Paftor of the Church of CHRIST in *Northampton.*

Amos ix 2, 3. *Though they dig into Hell, thence fhall
mine Hand take them ; though they climb up to Heaven,
thence will I bring them down. And though they hide
themfelves in the Top of Carmel, I will fearch and take
them out thence ; and though they be hid from my Sight
in the Bottom of the Sea, thence I will command the
Serpent, and he fhall bite them.*

The Second Edition.

ᵗ T O N : Printed and Sold by S. KNEELAND
ᵗ. GREEN in Queen-Street over againft the
1 7 4 2.

Sinners in the Hands of an Angry God, *a stirring and poetic sermon delivered by Jonathan Edwards in Connecticut in 1741, was published in book form in 1742.*

shadow," she remembered, "Peace of Mind seemed to be my Portion. . . . once I was blind. I hope now I see."

Doubting, quaking, repenting, swooning; believing, floating, swimming, leaping, dancing: conversion was a deeply felt mental and *physical* experience for the multitude of female converts who renewed their covenant with God during the mid-century awakenings. And while the steps on the road to conversion were familiar ones (17th-century accounts centered on the same themes of repentance and renewal), these female converts were also forging a new path. Forgotten, for a time, was the belief that women had to keep silent in church. Suddenly their expressions of heavenly delight were heard everywhere. In a movement that elevated emotion over intellect there was no "weaker" sex; female converts became, in many respects, the equals of men. Would not Anne Hutchinson (by then a century dead) have exulted to see New England's ministers at last agree with her assessment: that women and men were "all one in Jesus Christ?"

But if women's conversion experiences in the mid-1700s enlarged traditional boundaries confining female piety, the Great Awakening also illustrated other forces at work in society. More than simply an expansion of the sphere inhabited by pious women, the revivals also testified to the extent to which provincial society was becoming fragmented. Old allegiances (one church, one established minister, one unquestioned loyalty) were yielding to new choices. Long-held beliefs in deference before authority and devotion to a single, common good was giving way in the face of new realities as the colonies grew and became more diverse. With the expansion of society came a new ability to decide one's fate, particularly in matters of religion.

But growth also created new divisions in colonial society. The struggle between old and new styles of preaching was just one among a number of emerging fissures within the population: there were also growing gaps between rich and poor, black and white, town and country. Along with a new equality in the religious experiences of pious men and women, the second quarter of the 18th century saw an increase in the disparity between male and female lives—and between the lives of some women and the lives of others.

If, by the middle of the 18th century, Salem, Massachusetts, was becoming a place of haves and have-nots, Mary Vial Holyoke certainly numbered among the haves. Her father, a prosperous merchant from Boston, had succeeded in his efforts to marry his daughter to a man worthy of her station: a physician and part-time poet always included in Salem's elite circles.

Together, Mary and Edward Holyoke were in a position to take advantage of all that the bustling port of Salem had to offer. The profits of Edward's trade gave them plenty of cash with which to purchase the increasingly diverse array of imported goods for sale in local shops. Unlike the majority of Essex County residents, the Holyokes had a gilt-framed mirror, full sets of table linens, and even some of those most modern of innovations: dining forks. Mary Holyoke's appearance too, reflected her status. Gold buttons, aprons of fine cambric cloth, lace petticoats, and even imported silks might have ornamented her everyday attire.

A flowered silk dress worn by Mrs. Sarah Clarke of Salem around 1760. Such fancy apparel was available only to the wealthy.

Not only her material goods, but also Mary Holyoke's role as housewife was shaped by her social station and by the place and time in which she lived. Many of her duties were different from the habits of earlier colonial goodwives—and different from the chores of local women whose means were more modest. Above all, her everyday life was increasingly separate from the world of men. As urban gentlemen like Edward Holyoke embarked on careers that took them further afield, their homes came to be dominated by their wives and children.

Was Mary Holyoke the sort of woman whom Benjamin Franklin derided in a 1727 letter to his sister as "only a pretty gentlewoman"— one more comfortable perched beside a fancy tea-table than setting to work at a spinning wheel? Her life was far more complex than the crude distinction Franklin drew between "pretty gentlewoman" and "good housewife" allows. Though she and her husband had time to attend local dances and teas, Mary Holyoke spent most of her time hard at work. Her diary entries from the 1760s describe days full of washing and ironing, planting herbs and vegetables, making soap and preserving bacon, and sewing—chores she might well have performed a century before. Though she had servants to help her with many of these tasks, her days remained long and arduous.

But Mary Holyoke also had the leisure and the means to think about more than just subsistence—more than food and shelter. She devoted herself to transforming her house into a genteel home, aspiring to standards of comfort that would have been unattainable when the local economy was less mature and which remained beyond the reach of her less well-to-do neighbors. Not content with the merely practical, women like Mary Holyoke tried to bring a small measure of English-style refinement and polish to their homes in the provinces. As she noted in her diary, she "put up the Chintz" hangings around her bed, and "hung pictures" to ornament her walls. She sent silks to England to be dyed—perhaps knowing that people she passed on the narrow streets of Salem would recognize the vivid hues of her dress as colors only London shops could produce. Indeed, she purchased many things her grandmother would have made by hand.

Still, life was no debutante ball for Mary Holyoke. One November she made time in her hectic schedule to churn and set aside 77

A page from the diary of Mary Holyoke for January 1795. The diary reveals that her days were filled with a mixture of hard work and social visits with her neighbors.

pounds of butter for the winter. She—not her husband or her servants—butchered a 164-pound pig and cut more than 1,800 asparagus stalks from her vegetable garden. In other words, women like Mary Holyoke did not live the life of the "housewife" or that of the "gentlewoman," but rather a kind of hybrid that incorporated parts of *both* popular stereotypes. She might take tea with her friends in the afternoon after spending the morning up to her elbows in brine "put[ting] beef in pickle." She might be skilled at embroidery, but her nimble fingers would not shrink from the less "feminine" work of dressing a calf's head.

Nonetheless, most women in the 18th-century would doubtlessly—and rightly—have envied Mary Holyoke. Though she and her circle could hardly be called a new leisure class, they lived more graciously than the vast majority of poor and middling farm wives in New

England and the middle colonies. For families like the Holyokes, life got easier as the colonial period wore on.

For many more humble families, the aging of the colonies meant a declining standard of living. As New England's population exploded, jumping from 100,000 in 1700 to roughly 400,000 by 1750, more people had to make do with less, particularly where land was concerned. In older towns like Dedham and Ipswich and Watertown, five generations of children were cramming themselves onto ever-smaller plots. In 1650, the average farming family subsisted on what they could grow on a 150-acre lot. By 1750, the average had shrunk to one-third that size—barely enough to sustain a family, let alone turn a profit. In the middle colonies, large numbers of new immigrants found themselves with no land at all, working as paid laborers and living as tenants on the growing farms of local agricultural entrepreneurs.

For parents and children alike, this state of affairs presented a crisis. Mary Holyoke's father had the resources necessary to secure a suitable match for his daughters. But with diminishing stores of land, most parents had little to promise their children. And without a prize of land and cash to extend to dutiful sons or a hefty dowry to bestow upon obedient daughters, fathers also had less control over

As New England's white population increased dramatically in the first half of the 18th century, some families found themselves sharing a home with older generations. Here, artist Benjamin West portrays three generations of his family under the same roof.

their children's decisions. After 1730, an increasing percentage of young women in New England appear to have married without their parents' consent. Rates of premarital pregnancy approached 40 percent by the 1750s. And ever larger numbers of young women married out of birth order, not waiting for their older sisters to find mates. In this sense, poorer women may have exerted a greater degree of control over their own lives in the 18th century than their mothers and grandmothers could have dreamt of in the 17th.

But in other respects their lives were becoming harder rather than easier. Most ordinary farm wives continued to eke out a hardscrabble existence on the eve of the American Revolution—and well beyond it. This, at least, was the way Ruth Belknap seemed to feel about her life in Dover, New Hampshire. Married to a local parson, Belknap was a literate goodwife, hardly among the poorest colonial women. Yet she took umbrage at the way some of her wealthier, more urban counterparts lived. There was nothing genteel, she knew, about the life she lived in Dover. In her 1782 poem, "The Pleasures of a Country Life," Belknap tried to tell women like Mary Holyoke and men like Benjamin Franklin how the other half lived:

> Ye starch'd up folks that live in town,
> That lounge upon your beds till noon,
> That never tire yourselves with work,
> Unless with handling knife & fork,
> Come, see the sweets of country life,
> Display'd in Parson B[elknap's] wife.

"Sweets," indeed! Belknap's poem dwells on the many chores that filled her hours from dawn to midnight. In 1750 as in 1650, the average farm wife's day was much as Belknap portrayed it: A house "with all confusion fill'd." Hands blistered by days filled with "toil and sweat." Perhaps the greatest difference between Belknap's life and that of her great-grandmother was not so much the content of her days as their *context*. In her grandmother's day, almost every woman had this sort of schedule. Now, it seemed, the wealthy few were setting standards that the poorer many simply could not afford to uphold. For women like Ruth Belknap, the conspicuous presence of local elites could make days on the farm seem long indeed.

The social and economic rifts that divided the population of 18th-century New England—the distinctions between a Mary Holyoke

For Mary Randolph Cary (1727-1781), the wife of a wealthy Virginia planter, life was made easier by the constant toil of slaves on her plantation and in her home.

and a Ruth Belknap—would have appeared almost invisible to Eliza Lucas. For the cleavages separating the haves from the have-nots in her world were so profound as to make most women in New England and the mid-Atlantic colonies seem roughly equal in comparison. Lucas's perspective, unlike Holyoke's and Belknap's, was forged in the plantation south: a world in which social distinctions were literally measured in black and white.

Born on the sugar island of Antigua in 1722, Eliza was the eldest daughter of planter aristocrat George Lucas. Schooled in London, Eliza returned to Antigua at the age of 15, every inch the English lady: fluent in French, well-read in the literature of the day, accomplished in music, and skillful with embroidery. In 1738, the Lucas family moved from the West Indies to South Carolina to take over some properties Eliza's paternal grandfather had bequeathed them. Eliza quickly became the toast of Charleston, then a lively city with nearly 7,000 inhabitants. Taking her place among the town's gentry, Eliza was feted at private balls, plied with such delicacies as oyster soup and venison, and paired for dances with dashing young naval officers. Little wonder she felt, as she noted in a letter to an English friend, that Carolinians "live very Genteel and very much in the English taste."

Soon after her arrival in South Carolina, however, Eliza Lucas's life took a dramatic turn. When the sudden outbreak of hostilities between England and Spain forced George Lucas to return to Antigua, he left Eliza to manage his three plantations. This was a considerable task, for these were not small family farms. Wappoo, the plantation on which Eliza and her family lived some 17 miles west of Charleston, spanned 600 acres. The other two were considerably larger: a plantation of 1,500 acres and another encompassing nearly 3,000 acres. These were immense capitalist enterprises—factories in the fields staffed with gangs of enslaved black workers. And Eliza, not yet 17 years old, became their mistress.

"I have the business of 3 plantations to transact," she wrote to her good friend in May 1740. The enterprise, she said, "requires much writing and more business and fatigue of other sorts than you can imagine." But with her education and extraordinary acumen, Eliza Lucas proved equal to the task. She introduced a variety of new crops to the plantation, experimenting with ginger, cotton, and figs before striking gold—or rather, blue—with indigo. With the help of agricultural innovators like Lucas, this dark blue dye favored in British textiles soon joined rice as one of the region's most profitable export crops.

In 1744, Eliza Lucas married a close family friend, Charles Pinckney, a prominent lawyer. With Charles frequently away on business in Charleston, she continued her agricultural experiments, overseeing the cultivation of flax and hemp on his properties. She also threw herself into the many duties of mothering the couple's four children. This job, as she saw it, was a complex one. No longer was it sufficient for a planter's wife—at least for one of Eliza Lucas Pinckney's stature—to merely ensure her children's survival. Among the wealthy, every aspect of children's lives was considered a matter for maternal concern. Eliza's papers include an evocative passage describing her thoughts on child care. She resolved, she wrote,

> to be a good Mother to my children, to pray for them, to set them good examples, to give them good advice, to be careful both of their souls and bodies. . . . and to instill piety, Virtue and true religion into them; to spare no paines or trouble to do them good.

We can assume that she accomplished her goals. By the time she succumbed to breast cancer in 1793, Eliza Lucas Pinckney had lived to see her daughter marry and prosper and her two surviving sons become important public officials in the young United States.

What allowed Eliza Lucas to "spare no paines or trouble" with her children? The answer, in large measure, was the work of female slaves. The growth of plantation slavery was the ever-present backdrop to each of Lucas's many accomplishments. To say that Eliza Lucas would have been aware of slavery is a gross understatement. In the West Indies and later in South Carolina, she lived in a world where African Americans comprised a majority of the population. Fully half of Charleston's 7,000 inhabitants were enslaved blacks. Colonywide, the population in the second quarter of the 18th century was roughly 65 percent black.

Though African Americans were a constant presence in her life, Eliza Lucas rarely commented on the institution of slavery. Her letters made no mention, for example, of the Stono Rebellion, a 1739 insurrection of some 80 slaves from Angola that erupted less than five miles from the Lucas homestead at Wappoo. Yet in all kinds of everyday ways, the institution of slavery made her life what it was.

This is not to say that Eliza Lucas and others like her were particularly cruel mistresses. Indeed, Lucas wrote with pride of the time she spent working with "two little black girls who I teach to read." But regardless of the small steps Lucas made to acknowledge the humanity of the enslaved women who worked for her, it was their labor that made her plantation run. Slave women working in the fields put into practice the agricultural experiments she devised. (Indeed, the familiarity of many blacks with the delicate cultivation of rice and indigo—crops grown in many parts of West Africa—provided expertise Anglo Americans lacked.) Slave women cooked Eliza Lucas's dinner and saw to the needs of her visitors. Slave women nursed her children, forced to set aside the needs of their own offspring in the process.

In this sense, Eliza Lucas Pinckney was both an extraordinary woman and an example of her times. Unusually learned and independent, she had opportunities few southern women did. But, like many wealthy southern women, she gained her independence by enslaving other women and men. Like New England and the middle colonies, the Chesapeake and the Carolinas were fast becoming a world of the few and the many. But in the mid-18th-century South, the few were always white and free, and the many, increasingly, were black slaves.

Perhaps nowhere in the British colonies would signs of the widening gulf between the few and the many have been as visible as in the port cities of New York, Boston, and Philadelphia. From the European perspective, these urban villages hardly deserved to be called "cities" at all. London in the mid-18th century was home to over half a million people, while Philadelphia, the largest of the colonial

A view of the busy harbor of Philadelphia in 1754. In the mid-18th century, this was the largest and most modern city in British North America.

American cities, had just 35,000 inhabitants on the eve of the Revolution.

Although less than 5 percent of the population of the future United States lived in these urban environments, they represented in many ways the cutting edge of social change. It was in the port cities that thousands of new immigrants lived side by side with Anglo Americans, enslaved African Americans, and a growing free black community. It was in the port cities that merchants of the middling sort became men of great wealth. And, at the same time, it was in the port cities that wage labor, landlessness, and abject poverty first became realities for many. The two developments, of course, were related. As in the plantation south, great fortunes were built upon the labor of those less fortunate. Dock workers, roustabouts, and domestic servants in New York and Philadelphia were typically not enslaved. But freedom meant little when wages were too low to put food on the table.

Women dwelling in the urban ports found themselves on both sides of this widening gap between wealth and poverty. On the losing end were women whose situations were so desperate that they were forced to accept public charity. By the early decades of the 18th century, cities like Boston, New York, and Philadelphia had outgrown traditional mechanisms of caring for those in need. Poor women, particularly widows, could not always count on their extended families to help them make ends meet. Many of them found creative ways to bring in a modest income. By working as domestic servants in wealthy households or by taking boarders into their own homes, some women of modest means were able to keep themselves afloat. But others were forced to turn to almshouses like the ones founded in Philadelphia in 1730 and in New York in 1736.

Other women found in the port cities of the mid-18th century a world of expanding opportunities. For those who possessed needed skills and whose deceased husbands or fathers had left them considerable resources, urban life was full of possibilities. As so-called "she merchants" (widowed or unmarried traders) and workers in growing professions such as newspaper printing, women forged new paths for themselves and helped fuel booming urban economies.

The single or widowed "woman of affairs" was not an 18th-century invention. In the early years of the colonies, women like

Mary Spratt Provoost Alexander took advantage of the increased opportunities available to women in the thriving port cities by opening her own shop in New York.

Margaret Brent of Maryland, an unmarried, highly educated woman whose family numbered among the inner circle of the colony's proprietor, Lord Baltimore, sometimes exercised considerable power in extraordinary circumstances. Brent, who, with her sister Mary, presided over an extensive plantation known as the "Sisters' Freehold" in St. Mary's City, won widespread praise for her business acumen during the colony's early years.

A century later, America's urban port towns were home to many latter-day Margaret Brents. Like Brent, most of the women who ran shops, traded, and otherwise made names for themselves as women of affairs had no husbands. Many were so-called "spinsters," part of the increasing percentage of Anglo-American women choosing never to marry. Others were widows of wealthy merchants or established artisans who expanded their economic roles after their husbands' deaths. Advertisements appearing in colonial newspapers from the 1720s to 1800 show the incredible variety of occupations pursued by such women. They touted their services as teachers, cooks, seamstresses, embroiderers, and vendors of commodities ranging from fine wines to farm equipment. Sarah Kemble Knight was one widow of means for whom the booming economy of the colonial ports meant opportunity. Born in 1666 to a Boston merchant and his wife, she was 22 years old when she wed Thomas Knight, a shipmaster who sailed out of Boston harbor. Unlike most women of her era, she gave birth to only one child—a fact which may have greatly expanded the amount of time she had to devote to matters beyond her daily round of housekeeping and childrearing duties.

Like many women in the 18th-century port towns, Knight played a variety of roles in the local economy. Proficient in reading and writing and familiar with the popular literature of her day, she turned these skills into a job as one of the growing number of young women who picked up a few extra pennies each week by teaching penmanship and reading to local children. Knight's vocation would take on heightened importance for women in the years after the American Revolution.

But Knight was not only teacher, mother, and mistress of her household. She was also a boardinghouse operator, taking in modest rents from up to half a dozen relatives and others who shared her large Boston home. She was a shopkeeper, running a small retail

AGNES LIND, MILLINER,

Hath just imported in the Prince of Wales, Capt. Curling, from London, a new assortment of millinery and other goods, viz.

BROWN taffety,
Pink and blue mantuas,
Lutestrings,
Alamode,
Poplins,
Flowered dresdens,
Plain and figured mecklenets,
Gauze caps and fillets,
Silver stomachers & pompoons,
Gauze stomachers with ditto,
Plain and flowered sattin cardinals,
Plain and figured silk palomonse,
Womens and girls scarlet cardinals,
Scarlet cloaks and quilted coats,
Womens and girls coloured and black sattin hats,
Sattin shoes,
Plain and figured ribbons,
Dresden and pinked handkerchiefs,
Head lace and footing,
Fine India chintzes,
White & coloured callicoes,
Clear and long lawns,
Britannias and Pomerantias,
Pistol lawns and silesias,
Men & boys castor & felt hats,
White and black glazed mitts,
Coloured, wash leather, and sattin ditto,
Clouting dieper,
Irish shirting and sheeting linen,
Blue and green plains,
Swanskin,
Blue and white linsey,
Men and womens worsted stockings,
Womens & girls plain, pink do.

Thread and cotton ditto.
Boys caps with black and white feathers
Crucls and canvas,
Fine hyson tea,
Green and bohea tea,
Durham mustard,
Pigtail and cut tobacco,
High and low toast snuff,
Short and long pipes,
Womens and girls everlasting shoes,
Red, black, plain and toed clogs,
Men and womens leather shoes,
Dresden and stock tape,
Holland and diaper ditto,
Broad tape and bobbins,
Silk and cotton laces,
Silk, cotton and thread mitts,
White and coloured same,
Pins, patches, and silks.
Sets of necklaces and ear-rings,
Pearl and blue stone ditto,
Cinnamon, nutmers, cloves, mace, and black pepper.
Scented and plain hair powder,
Poland starch, & powder blue,
Wash balls and teeth powder,
Powder boxes and puff.
Fine enamell'd & japanned snuff boxes,
Fine India china in sets,
Enamelled and blue and white bowls,
Enamelled and blue and white coffe cups,
Enamelled and blue and white cups and saucers, tea-pots milk-pots, &c. &c.

GOOD West-India and Northward RUM,
Muscovado and loaf sugar, and a parcel of hams, per in bales, to be sold very reasonably, by Da Cusrs &...

Agnes Lind, a shopkeeper in Charleston, was one of the most persistent advertisers in the South-Carolina Gazette. This ad, which appeared on August 21, 1762, lists an assortment of goods that had just arrived in her store from London.

While Benjamin Franklin was away for months or years at a time on diplomatic missions, he left the running of his book and stationery business to his wife, Deborah Read Franklin.

establishment from her home. She was a traveler, striking out on her own in 1704 on an arduous five-month journey to New Haven and keeping a journal of the expedition for posterity. Though the ostensible purpose of the trip was to settle a kinswoman's estate, Knight found plenty of time to do some business along the way. She reported her success at a "vendue" or auction in New York, where she purchased 100 reams of fine Dutch paper at a price that would allow her a substantial profit. She was indeed, as she wrote in her travel journal, "fitt for business." At her death in 1727, she had parlayed the proceeds from her various enterprises into the considerable estate of £1,800.

Like the wives of many urban artisans, Deborah Read Franklin, wife of printer and future statesman Benjamin Franklin, contributed valuable skills to her husband's career. With Benjamin away for months or even years at a time on state business, Deborah Franklin looked after his book and stationary business at home in Philadelphia. In his *Autobiography*, Benjamin Franklin remembered his wife as "a good and faithful Helpmate" who "assisted me much by attending the shop." Such a helpmate, he knew, was indispensable in his rapidly changing world. As he noted in a letter to a male friend in 1745, marriage had become a necessity for the enterprising man. "It is the Man and Woman united that make the compleat human Being," he wrote. "Together they are more likely to succeed in the World." In the commercial environment of 18th-century Philadelphia, success in one's profession had become the measure of a man. This kind of success, Franklin knew, was hard to attain without the help of a wife with a good head for business.

Did the male leaders of these colonial port cities recognize the value of the work performed by women like Sarah Kemble Knight and Deborah Read Franklin? What, for that matter, did these urban women of affairs think of their own contributions? Few 18th-century men and women pondered such questions in their diaries and letters. But the petition a group of New York's female traders addressed to newspaper editor John Peter Zenger in 1733 reveals that at least *some* urban women were aware of their importance to the local economy—and that they were beginning to chafe against the second-class status accorded to female workers. "Mr. Zenger," they wrote, "We, the widdows of this city, have had a Meeting, and as our case is something Deplorable, we beg you will give [our petition a] Place in your *Weekly Journal* . . . it is as follows":

> We are House keepers, Pay our Taxes, carry on Trade, and most of us are she Merchants, and as we in some measure contribute to the Support of Government, we ought to be Intitled to some of the Sweets of it; but we find ourselves entirely neglected, while the Husbands that live in our Neighborhood are daily invited to Dine at Court; we have the Vanity to think we can be full[y] as Entertaining, and make as brave a Defence in Case of an Invasion and perhaps not turn Tail so soon as some of them.

We do not know what the *Journal*'s readers made of this striking request. They may have found these protestations of bravery in the face of an invasion outlandish indeed. After all, no foreign invasion or domestic insurrection was then visible on the horizon. Within a generation, however, the ability of women like New York's "she Merchants" to conduct themselves as loyal and prosperous Americans would become essential to the colonies' claims to stand as a nation. For it was amid the political turmoil of the 1760s and 1770s that American women's lives would first become a topic of heated public debate.

KEEP WITHIN COMPASS.

BE SURE, TO AVOID MANY TROUBLES WHICH OTHERS ENDURE KEEP WITHIN COMPASS AND YOU SHALL

FEAR GOD

PRUDENCE

PRODUCETH ESTEEM.

Published as the Act directs, 16 Aug 1785.

WHAT THEN IS THE AMERICAN, THIS NEW WOMAN?

In 1782 Hector St. John de Crèvecouer, a Frenchman who had made his home in New York since the 1760s, set out to document for European readers something of the feel of life in the young United States. His *Letters From An American Farmer* tells the story of a people who had declared their independence from England only six years before and had yet to achieve a final military victory over British forces. From Crèvecoeur's perspective, the American story was, above all, a tale of newness and of oneness: the story of a recently created society made up of disparate individuals working toward a shared dream of the future. The traveler who first set eyes on this strange new country, Crèvecouer wrote, beholds "an immense country . . . where an hundred years ago all was wild."

Who, Crèvecouer wanted to discover, were the architects of this "modern society" lately sprung up in the wilderness? How had what he termed a "promiscuous breed" of people—"a mixture of English, Scotch, Irish, French, Dutch, Germans, and Swedes" (along with populations of Native Americans and African Americans whom Crèvecouer failed to notice)—come together as a single political entity? He hoped his journeys would help him to answer the ultimate riddle of the American national character: "What then is the American, this new man?"

This 18th-century engraving advises women that "Prudence Produceth Esteem." Those who might be tempted to test the limits of a woman's role in 18th-century society were reminded to "Keep Within Compass And You Shall be Sure To Avoid Many Troubles Which Others Endure."

The poet Phillis Wheatley was initially purchased by the Wheatley family as a slave. She so impressed them with her intelligence and piety that they educated her and treated her, in the words of her mistress, like "a daughter." Although her poetry caught the attention of many prominent people in New England and abroad, she died in poverty at the age of 30.

Crèvecouer was not particularly interested in uncovering the character of the *female* members of what he described as "that race now called Americans." But his observations about the lives of American men point to important questions. How much had the lives of colonial American women changed from the beginnings of European settlement to the eve of the American Revolution more than 150 years later? To what extent did the experiences of the diverse kinds of women living in the colonies in, say, 1763, add up to a unified, almost national identity? As the British colonies began to edge slowly toward revolution, was there, as yet, anything particularly American about America's women?

Phillis Wheatley would have had mixed answers to these complicated questions. A young African woman born in the early 1750s and brought to Boston in chains in 1761, Wheatley knew the worst and the best of women's lives in the emerging nation. Legally, her status was that of a slave. Purchased by wealthy Boston cloth merchant John Wheatley and his wife Susannah, Phillis was one of the 250,000 to 300,000 Africans forcibly imported to North America in the 18th century. Yet Wheatley's lot was very different from the lives of most Africans and their American-born descendants. For Phillis demonstrated such extraordinary talents as a young girl that the family who owned her wound up raising her, her mistress later said, "as a daughter": schooling her in the classics; talking, reading, and praying with her.

Beginning with the publication of her first verse in a Rhode Island newspaper in 1767, Wheatley's poems celebrating republican virtue, a life of learning, and the redeeming power of God brought her to the attention of such luminaries as Thomas Jefferson, George Whitefield, John Hancock, and George Washington. But in the end, Wheatley's fame was fleeting. Although her poems expressed her passion for the triumph of American-style liberty over British tyranny, and although she extolled the accomplishments of slave-owning national heroes like George Washington, Phillis Wheatley remained on the sidelines of the freedom she celebrated.

Formally, she became a freedwoman in 1773 when her master signed a document releasing her from bondage. But in other ways she remained shackled: constrained no longer by slavery but by poverty. Married in 1778 to John Peters, an educated free black man living in

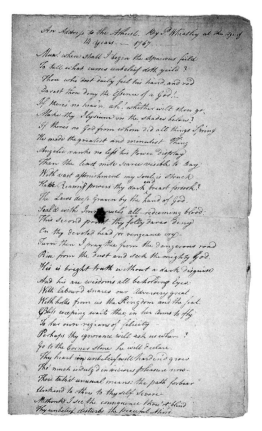

Phillis Wheatley wrote "An Address to the Atheist" when she was 14 years old. Bostonians were impressed with her piety and her learning.

Boston, she endured the kind of material deprivation experienced by many free blacks in the urban North. She continued to work on her poetry, but writing could not pay the bills. By 1784, all three of her children had died in infancy, her husband had landed in debtors' prison, and Phillis herself, aged 30, was consigned to a pauper's grave.

For the white New England women who belonged to the same evangelical religious circles as Phillis Wheatley and her mistress, there was much to celebrate in the second half of the 18th century. In the aftermath of the Great Awakening, female piety had become a force to be reckoned with. Recognized by male leaders for their devotion to matters spiritual, many newly "awakened" women began to extend their moral influence beyond the limits of their households.

Sarah Osborn was one of those who took full advantage of the possibilities for religious leadership afforded to some women at the end of the colonial period. Born Sarah Haggar in London in 1714, she arrived in the colonies with her parents in the early 1720s and settled in Newport, Rhode Island, in 1729. Married at the age of 18

SARAH OSBORN, Schoolmiftrefs in Newport,

propofes to keep a

Boarding School.

ANY Perfon defirous of fending Children, may be accommodated, and have them inftructed in Reading, Writing, Plain Work, Embroidering, Tent Stitch, Samplers, &c. on reafonable Terms

---

NEWPORT, RHODE-ISLAND :

and widowed before she reached 20, Sarah Haggar Wheaten made ends meet by teaching in a local dame school. Remarried in 1742 to a widower named Henry Osborn, she continued to work as a teacher for the rest of her long life. By 1758, when she began boarding pupils in her Newport home, the school had expanded to enroll more than 70 students. For most of her life, the income Osborn generated through her school was the sole support of her family.

It was around the time of her second marriage that Sarah Osborn first showed her skill at another sort of teaching: serving as a leader in the local religious community. Inspired, like so many others in the colonies, by the preaching of George Whitefield, she began to lead groups of local women in prayer. As she later wrote in an unpublished autobiography,

> a number of young women, who were awakened to a concern for their souls, came to me, and desired my advice and assistance, and proposed to join in a society; provided I would take care of them.

Like a latter-day Anne Hutchinson, Osborn met weekly with this pious group in her home. But if the format was much the same as that of Hutchinson's "conventicles," the times had changed. Unlike Puritan ministers in the 1630s, leading male preachers in the 1750s encouraged the initiative of laywomen like Osborn—up to a point.

By the 1760s, however, Osborn's prayer group had become a ministry in its own right. Every evening except Saturdays, crowds of men, women, and children gathered at her house for sessions of what she modestly termed "family worship." Sundays were devoted to the religious education of local slaves and free blacks—a group she called her "Ethiopian Society" that numbered as many as 90. In January 1767, Osborn reported, more than 525 people were flocking to her meetings each week. "I was affrighted at the throng," she wrote to Joseph Fish, a friend who was the minister of nearby Stonington, Connecticut, "and Greatly feared that it would be as the river Jordan overflowing all the banks." Fish's response was not encouraging, for he and other established ministers shared Osborn's distress. Though the specter of Anne Hutchinson had been consigned to the remote past, there were still some limits, the ministers made clear, on female piety. Osborn was treading perilously close to those limits. Teaching blacks, she might upset the precarious racial balance in town. Teaching men, she might transcend her role as wife and mother. Fish and others recommended that Osborn curb her ministerial duties and take up more feminine pursuits such as needlework and private prayer.

The more women's lives had changed, Fish's reaction seems to suggest, the more they had stayed the same. Or had they? For if the ministers' suggestions tried to remake Sarah Osborn to fit a traditional mold, her rebuttal hints at a new self-confidence among some American women. On the surface, at least, her tone was submissive enough. But after assuring Fish of her concern for "Moving beyond my line," she steadfastly defended her supposedly unfeminine activities. "Would you advise me to shut up my Mouth and doors and creep into obscurity?" she asked. She was not willing to do so. As Osborn understood the situation, she was doing only what God asked of her.

In the end, time solved Osborn's dilemma. By 1769 the prayer meetings in her home had shrunk to a size local male leaders apparently found acceptable. Yet Osborn's involvement in Newport's religious life remained undiminished. Her female prayer group continued to exert considerable power in church affairs long after Osborn's own health began to fail.

Elizabeth Sandwith, born to wealthy Quaker parents in Philadelphia in 1735, encountered a world much like Sarah Osborn's: a world in which expanding possibilities for women's lives mixed with continued limitations. Her father's prosperity as a merchant bought

Sarah Osborn kept a journal from shortly before her 30th birthday, in December 1743, until she died in 1796. After her death, Samuel Hopkins, the minister of the First Congregational Church in Newport and a close friend of Osborn's, published selections from her journal as Memoirs of the Life of Mrs. Sarah Osborn.

MEMOIRS

OF THE

L I F E

OF

MRS. SARAH OSBORN,

WHO DIED AT

NEWPORT, RHODEISLAND,

ON THE SECOND DAY OF AUGUST, 1796.

IN THE EIGHTY THIRD YEAR OF HER AGE.

BY SAMUEL HOPKINS, D. D.

PASTOR OF THE FIRST CONGREGATIONAL CHURCH IN NEWPORT.

PRINTED AT WORCESTER, MASSACHUSETTS,
BY LEONARD WORCESTER.
1799.

Elizabeth Drinker's diary, which she began keeping in 1758, covers her day-to-day life as she gave birth to nine children and struggled through her daily chores. Drinker's household was much involved in the political struggles of the day. During the American Revolution, she was forced to house a British officer while her husband was being held prisoner.

her many advantages, including the chance to study at one of Pennsylvania's most rigorous schools for young women. Married in 1761 to a prominent Quaker merchant named Henry Drinker, Elizabeth would spend her life surrounded by the finest things.

Although Elizabeth Drinker was not particularly observant in matters of religion, her family's Quaker traditions provided an important foundation for her life. Perhaps it was the Quakers, who believed that girls should be educated in a manner similar to boys and who welcomed female preaching, who gave Elizabeth her passion for self-expression. Beginning in 1758 she kept a diary faithfully for more than five decades, recording her thoughts on matters great and small. Her carefully handwritten manuscript fills nearly three dozen volumes.

Elizabeth Drinker's extensive journals reveal a life in which the mundane mixed with the extraordinary. Like most women of her era, her days were given over primarily to childbearing and child-rearing. She gave birth to nine children over the course of her marriage. Although Drinker had servants (and, in her youth, at least one slave) to help with her daily chores, it is little wonder that she was often, as she wrote in the diary, "very busy all day."

These aspects of Elizabeth Drinker's life echo the daily experience of women throughout the American colonies from the early 17th century on. Yet the political changes sweeping the continent in the 1760s and 1770s touched the Drinker household as they did so many others. The American Revolution literally broke down Elizabeth's front door in 1777, when she was forced to house a British officer while her husband was being held as a prisoner of war in Virginia.

Despite this unsentimental education in the ways of the world beyond the domestic, however, Elizabeth Drinker would continue to believe that her place was within her family. "I am not acquainted with the extent of my husband's great variety of engagements," she would note in her diary, confessing her ignorance of the affairs of men. "I stay much at home, and my business I mind," she wrote with pride.

In the winter of 1766 a woman we know only as Hannah made a decision that was in many ways more dramatic—even revolutionary —than even the most stirring moments in the lives of women like Elizabeth Drinker or Sarah Osborn. Hannah, a black woman of about 35 years of age, was a slave on the plantation of one Stephen Dence who decided, against all odds, to run away. The only record we have of her life comes from an advertisement he placed in the *Virginia Gazette* offering a reward for her capture.

What was Hannah's life like? Only the most rudimentary details of her toilsome existence survive. Small and light-skinned—"yellow," in Dence's description—she may have been the child of a slave mother and a white father, possibly even Dence himself. She had long hair, Dence wrote, perhaps to help cover the "many scars on her back, occasioned by whipping." She had rebelled before and had endured the punishment her owner meted out. But by December 15, she had reached the limits of her tolerance. Helped by "other Negroes" who leant her clothes for her journey, Hannah stole the only thing she owned: herself. Did the large-scale changes then taking place in the American colonies help her to make her courageous choice?

Perhaps, like Sarah Osborn and so many others, she, too, had been "awakened" by evangelical religion. Her former owner noted with disgust that "She pretends much to the religion the Negroes of late have practised." Perhaps, in addition, she had recently heard heated talk about the value of liberty. After all, Virginia, the colony whose laws enslaved her, was also one of the places where white men spoke most passionately about independence. We do not know whether such thoughts were running through Hannah's mind when she took flight on that bleak December morning, hoping, her master assumed, to "pass for a free woman" in some larger town to the South. But these thoughts were indeed on the minds of the tens of thousands of slaves who later took advantage of wartime disruptions to slip away in search of the freedom so many Americans were talking about.

How much had the lives of colonial American women changed by the winter of 1766–67—the winter during which Sarah Osborn preached to hundreds every week, the winter Hannah took flight in search of freedom? How new was Hector St. John de Crèvecouer's "new [wo]man"? In some ways, it seems, she was profoundly different from her 17th-century forebears. In other respects, she had hardly changed at all.

In 1767 as in 1607, most women in the colonies were not Quaker merchants' wives or urban school teachers or celebrated black po-

While the Second Continental Congress was meeting in Philadelphia in 1776, Abigail Adams, the wife of John Adams, a Patriot leader and future President of the United States, wrote to him and encouraged him to "Remember the Ladies" in the country's new code of laws.

ets. The vast majority, enslaved and free, were farm wives: giving birth to child after child after child, spending all their daylight hours (and more) doing backbreaking work. On the whole, their education remained inferior to that of their brothers. The authorities who presided over their lives, from town selectmen to the crown representatives, were, as they always had been, exclusively male.

And yet some women—especially those privileged enough to benefit from broader changes in colonial society—entered the era of the revolution with rising expectations. They were marrying whom and when they chose—and not marrying at all in increasing numbers. They were seeking divorces when their marriages became unbearable. They were not only listening to revival preaching, but delivering God's message themselves. They were fleeing cruel masters in search of a better life.

In the years ahead, some American women would try to change not only their own lives, but the status of women as a group. Abigail Smith Adams, wife of Massachusetts patriot leader John Adams, was one of the first to articulate this fervent hope. In a letter she wrote to her husband while he was away at the second Continental Congress in Philadelphia in 1776, she reminded him that women, too, were wrestling with the meaning of freedom:

> I long to hear that you have declared an independancy—and by the way in the new Code of Laws which I suppose it will be necessary for you to make I desire you would Remember the Ladies, and be more generous and favorable to them than your ancestors. Do not put such unlimited power in to the hands of the Husbands. Remember all Men would be tyrants if they could. If particular care and attention is not paid to the Ladies we are determined to foment a Rebellion, and will not hold ourselves bound by any laws in which we have no voice, or Representation.

John Adams answered by gently mocking his wife, calling her "saucy" and saying he could "not but laugh" at her request.

It would be a long time before American women did, as Abigail Adams threatened, "foment a rebellion." It would take longer still for women to gain the kinds of legal protections she asked for. Yet many women in the late 18th century were, like Abigail Adams, unwilling to continue to have "no voice" in public affairs. Certainly, they did not speak with a single voice. Sarah Osborn preached. Phillis Wheatley wrote verse. Elizabeth Drinker recorded her thoughts in a

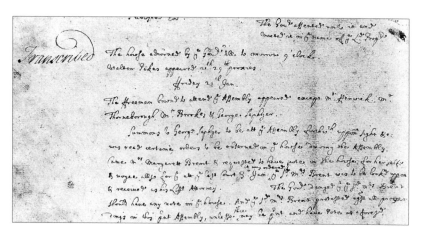

journal. Hannah "spoke" by running away. They did not all speak in the same tones, nor did they claim the same rights and prerogatives. But they spoke nonetheless, to whomever would listen: to their husbands, to male leaders in their churches and towns, and especially to each other.

But then again, American women had been claiming a voice in their communities' affairs long before there was any thought of a United States. "Came Mistress Margaret Brent and requested to have [a] vote in the house for her self, and [a] voice also." Margaret Brent, the wealthy Maryland planter, made her bumptious request before that colony's assembly in January 1648. The response recorded in the assembly's proceedings was predictable: "The Governor denied that the said Mistress Brent should have any vote in the house." But like Anne Hutchinson, Phillis Wheatley, Anne Bradstreet, Mary Dyer, and so many other nameless women in the North American colonies, Margaret Brent would not take no for an answer.

We should not imagine that women like Brent regarded themselves as feminists by the 20th century's definition. Brent was not demanding equal rights in general but a vote on the specific issue being considered that particular day in 1648. What is certain, though, is that Abigail Adams had a long tradition to fall back on when she gently challenged the "tyranny" of colonial husbands in 1776.

CHRONOLOGY

1607	English settlement of Jamestown
1608	French settlement of Québec
1610	Spanish settlement of Santa Fe
1619	First Africans brought to Chesapeake; Governor Edwyn Sandys begins importing English "wives" for Virginia
1620	Pilgrims found Plymouth colony
1629	Puritans found Massachusetts Bay colony
1630–42	Great migration to New England
1638	Anne Hutchinson banished from Massachusetts
1639	Marie Guyart founds Ursuline Convent in Québec City
1648	Margaret Brent demands a vote in Maryland's assembly
1650	A volume of Anne Bradstreet's poetry, *The Tenth Muse Lately Sprung Up in America*, is published in London
1659–60	Executions in Massachusetts of Quaker women
1660	Restoration of Charles II to the English throne
1662	New England Puritans enact Half-Way Covenant
1663	Carolina colony founded (divided 1691)
1664	English seize control of Dutch settlements in New Netherland
1675–76	King Philip's War/Metacom's Rebellion; Mary Rowlandson's captivity; Bacon's Rebellion
1681	Pennsylvania founded as Quaker haven
1688	Glorious Revolution in England
1689–97	King William's War
1692	Salem witchcraft trials
1702–13	Queen Anne's War

1704	Deerfield Massacre—Eunice Williams captured; Sarah Kemble Knight's journey from Boston to New York
1730s–1760s	Great Awakening
1739	War of Jenkins' Ear begins (ends 1742); Stono Rebellion in South Carolina; Eliza Lucas begins managing three South Carolina plantations
1739, 1741	Itinerant preacher George Whitefield tours North American colonies
1743	Conversion of Sarah Pierpont Edwards
1744–48	King George's War
1757–63	French and Indian War (Seven Years' War)
1767	Phillis Wheatley's first poem published; Sarah Osborn holds mass revival meetings in her Massachusetts home

FURTHER READING

A Note on Sources

In the interest of readability, the volumes in this series include no discussion of historiography and no footnotes. As works of synthesis and overview, however, they are greatly indebted to the research and writing of other historians. The principal works drawn on in this volume are among the books listed below.

General Histories of the Colonial Period

Axtell, James. *The European and the Indian: Essays in the Ethnohistory of Colonial North America*. New York: Oxford University Press, 1981.

Bailyn, Bernard. *The Peopling of British North America: An Introduction*. New York: Vintage, 1986.

Bonomi, Patricia. *Under the Cope of Heaven: Religion, Society, and Politics in Colonial America*. New York: Oxford University Press, 1986.

Boyer, Paul, and Stephen Nissenbaum. *Salem Possessed: The Social Origins of Witchcraft*. Cambridge: Harvard University Press, 1974.

Cooke, Jacob Ernest, et al., eds. *Encyclopedia of the North American Colonies*. 3 vols. New York: Scribners, 1993.

Fischer, David Hackett. *Albion's Seed: Four British Folkways in America*. New York: Oxford University Press, 1989.

Innes, Stephen, ed. *Work and Labor in Early America*. Chapel Hill: University of North Carolina Press, 1988.

Kulikoff, Allan. *Tobacco and Slaves: The Development of Southern Cultures in the Chesapeake, 1680–1800*. Chapel Hill: University of North Carolina Press, 1986.

Lockridge, Kenneth A. *A New England Town: The First Hundred Years*. New York: Norton, 1970.

Morgan, Edmund S. *American Slavery, American Freedom: The Ordeal of Colonial Virginia*. New York: Norton, 1975.

————. *The Puritan Dilemma: The Story of John Winthrop*. Boston: Little, Brown, 1958.

Rutman, Darrett B., and Anita H. Rutman. *A Place in Time: Middlesex County, Virginia, 1650–1750*. New York: Norton, 1984.

Sobel, Mechal. *The World They Made Together: Black and White Values in Eighteenth-Century Virginia*. Princeton, N.J.: Princeton University Press, 1987.

Tate, Thad W., and David L. Ammerman. *The Chesapeake in the Seventeenth Century: Essays on Anglo-American Society*. Chapel Hill: University of North Carolina Press, 1979.

Weber, David J. *The Spanish Frontier in North America*. New Haven: Yale University Press, 1992.

White, Richard. *The Middle Ground: Indians, Empires, and Republics in the Great Lakes Region, 1650–1815.* New York: Cambridge University Press, 1991.

Wood, Peter S. *Black Majority: Negroes in Colonial South Carolina from 1670 through the Stono Rebellion.* New York: Norton, 1974.

Women, Family, and Household in Early America

Boydston, Jeanne. *Home and Work: Housework, Wages, and the Ideology of Labor in the Early Republic.* New York: Oxford University Press, 1990.

D'Emilio, John, and Estelle B. Freedman. *Intimate Matters: A History of Sexuality in America.* New York: Harper & Row, 1988.

Demos, John. *A Little Commonwealth: Family Life in Plymouth Colony.* New York: Oxford University Press, 1970.

Devens, Carol. *Countering Colonization: Native American Women and the Great Lakes Missions.* Berkeley: University of California Press, 1992.

Earle, Alice Morse. *Colonial Dames and Good Wives.* 1895. Reprint. Bowie, Md.: Heritage Books, 1988.

———. *Margaret Winthrop.* 1895. Reprint. Williamstown, Mass.: Corner House, 1975.

Greven, Philip. *The Protestant Temperament: Patterns of Child-Rearing, Religious Experience, and the Self in Early America.* Chicago: University of Chicago Press, 1977.

Gutiérrez, Ramón A. *When Jesus Came, the Corn Mothers Went Away: Marriage, Sexuality, and Power in New Mexico, 1500–1846.* Stanford, Calif.: Stanford University Press, 1991.

Hoffman, Ronald, and Peter J. Albert, eds. *Women in the Age of the American Revolution.* Charlottesville: University of Virginia Press, 1989.

Jones, Jacqueline. *Labor of Love, Labor of Sorrow: Black Women, Work, and the Family, from Slavery to the Present.* New York: Vintage, 1986.

Karlsen, Carol F. *The Devil in the Shape of a Woman: Witchcraft in Colonial New England.* New York: Norton, 1987.

Koehler, Lyle. *A Search for Power: The "Weaker Sex" in Seventeenth-Century New England.* Urbana: University of Illinois Press, 1980.

Morgan, Edmund S. *The Puritan Family: Religion and Domestic Relations in Seventeenth-Century New England.* New York: Harper & Row, 1966.

Narrett, David E. *Inheritance and Family Life in Colonial New York City.* Ithaca, N.Y.: Cornell University Press, 1992.

Norton, Mary Beth. *Liberty's Daughters: The Revolutionary Experience of American Women.* Boston: Little, Brown, 1980.

Salmon, Marylynn. *Women and the Law of Property in Early America.* Chapel Hill: University of North Carolina Press, 1986.

Smith, Daniel Blake. *Inside the Great House: Planter Family Life in Eighteenth-Century Chesapeake Society.* Ithaca, N.Y.: Cornell University Press, 1980.

Spruill, Julia C. *Women's Life and Work in the Southern Colonies.* 1938. Reprint. New York: Norton, 1972.

Thompson, Roger. *Sex in Middlesex: Popular Mores in a Massachusetts County, 1649–1699.* Amherst: University of Massachusetts Press, 1986.

Ulrich, Laurel T. *Good Wives: Image and Reality in the Lives of Women in Northern New England, 1650–1750*. New York: Knopf, 1982.

Wall, Helena M. *Fierce Communion: Family and Community in Early America*. Cambridge: Harvard University Press, 1990.

Woodward, Grace Steele. *Pocahontas*. Norman: University of Oklahoma Press, 1969.

Primary Sources by or about Early American Women

Andrews, William L., ed. *Journeys in New Worlds: Early American Women's Narratives*. Madison: University of Wisconsin Press, 1990.

Axtell, James, ed. *The Indian Peoples of Eastern America: A Documentary History of the Sexes*. New York: Oxford University Press, 1981.

Boyer, Paul, and Stephen Nissenbaum. *Salem Village Witchcraft: A Documentary Record of Local Conflict in Colonial New England*. Boston: Northeastern University Press, 1993.

Crane, Elaine Forman, ed. *The Diary of Elizabeth Drinker*. 3 vols. Boston: Northeastern University Press, 1991.

Hall, David D., ed. *The Antinomian Controversy, 1636–1638: A Documentary History*. 2nd ed. Durham, N.C.: Duke University Press, 1990.

———. *Witch-Hunting in Seventeenth-Century New England: A Documentary History, 1638–1692*. Boston: Northeastern University Press, 1991.

Hensley, Jeannine, ed. *The Works of Anne Bradstreet*. Cambridge: Harvard University Press, 1967.

Karlsen, Carol F., and Laurie Crumpacker, eds. *The Journal of Esther Edwards Burr, 1754–1757*. New Haven: Yale University Press, 1984.

Pinckney, Elise, ed. *The Letter Book of Eliza Lucas Pinckney, 1739–1762*. Chapel Hill: University of North Carolina Press, 1972.

Ruether, Rosemary R., and Rosemary S. Keller, eds. *Women and Religion in America: A Documentary History*. Vol. 2, *The Colonial and Revolutionary Periods*. New York: Harper & Row, 1983.

Shields, John, ed. *The Collected Works of Phillis Wheatley*. New York: Oxford University Press, 1988.

INDEX

Picture Credits

American Antiquarian Society: 20, 115; American Philosophical Society: 138 bottom, 138 top; the Bettmann Archive: 70; Boston Athenaeum: 92; by courtesy of the Trustees of the Boston Public Library: 67 left; the British Library: 26, 44; the Charleston Museum, Charleston, South Carolina: 40; Colonial Williamsburg: 58, 140; by permission of the Folger Shakespeare Library: 80; courtesy of the Harvard University Portrait Collection, gift of Mrs. H. P. Oliver to Harvard College, 1852: 122 left; Historical Society of Pennsylvania: 54, 90, 99, 122 right, 146; by permission of the Houghton Library, Harvard University: 57, 67 right (MS Am 1007.1), 81; the Huntington Library, Rare Book Department: 114; Iroquois Indian Museum, Howes Cave, New York: 75, 77; Paul Leibe/Historic St. Mary's City: 35; Library Company of Philadelphia: 39, 121, 134; Library of Congress: 13, 18, 30, 36, 42, 45, 48, 52 right, 52 left, 59, 79, 83, 85, 86, 87, 93, 98, 101, 105 left, 105 right, 137, 142; Longmeadow Historical Society, Longmeadow, Mass.: 62; Maryland State Archives: 149; Massachusetts Historical Society: 21, 82, 106, 117, 143, 148; © McCord Museum of Canadian History, Montreal: 19, 28; Metropolitan Museum of Art: 55 (Rogers Fund, 1913. 13.69.45), 118 (Gift of Mrs. J. Insley Blair, 1946. 46.194.2b); Museum of the City of New York. *Mary Spratt Provoost Alexander*, by John Wollaston, accession number 50.215.4: 135; Museum of Fine Arts, Houston, the Bayou Bend Collection, gift of Miss Ima Hogg: 65; Museum of New Mexico: 7 (#52883/13), 78 (#83028); from the collection of the Newport Historical Society: 144, 145; Collection of the New-York Historical Society: 23, 60, 88; New York Public Library, Rare Book Room, Astor, Lenox, and Tilden Foundations: 24; 33, 56, 125; courtesy Peabody Essex Museum, Salem, Massachusetts: 50, 51, 64, 116, 127, 129; The Art Museum, Princeton University. Gift of Snowden Henry: 130; St. Francis Xavier Mission (Blessed Kateri Shrine), Kahnawake, Quebec: 72; Smithsonian Institution: 17 left (#81-11470), 17 right (#86-11552); State Historical Society of North Dakota: 16; University of New Hampshire, University Library, Special Collections Department: 103; University of Virginia, Alderman Library: 111; Virginia State Library and Archives: frontispiece, 10, 12, 14, 25, 32, 96, 109, 113, 132; Wethersfield Historical Society, Wethersfield, Connecticut: 47; courtesy Winterthur Museum: 63; Worcester Art Museum, Worcester, Massachusetts. Gift of Mr. and Mrs. Albert W. Rice: cover; Yale University Art Gallery: 120 (gift of Hon. Jonathan Edwards, B.A. 1819), 123 (bequest of Eugene Phelps Edwards).

Acknowledgments

I would like to thank Sarah E. Redfield for her invaluable and cheerful assistance with background research for this project.

In addition to the works previously cited, a number of excellent articles were essential to this volume. See especially the following: Clara Sue Kidwell, "Indian Women as Cultural Mediators," *Ethnohistory*, vol. 39, no. 2 (Spring 1992), 98–107; Antonia I. Castañeda, "Gender, Race, and Culture: Spanish-Mexican Women in the Historiography of Frontier California," *Frontiers*, vol. 11, no. 1 (1990), 8–20, and "Sexual Violence in the Politics and Policies of Conquest: Amerindian Women and the Spanish Conquest of Alta California," in Adela de la Torre and Beatriz M. Pesquera, eds., *Building With Our Own Hands: New Directions in Chicana Studies* (Berkeley: University of California Press, 1993), 15–33; Carol Shammas, "Black Women's Work and the Evolution of Plantation Society in Virginia," *Labor History*, vol. 26, no. 1 (1985), 7–28; Susan Westbury, "Women in Bacon's Rebellion," in Virginia Bernhard et al., eds., *Southern Women: Histories and Identities* (Columbia: University of Missouri Press, 1992), 30–46; Mary Beth Norton, "'My Resting Reaping Times:' Sarah Osborne's Defense of Her 'Unfeminine' Activities, 1767," *Signs: Journal of Women in Culture and Society*, vol. 2, no. 2 (Winter 1976), 515–29.

A note on spelling: For the sake of clarity and readability, variant spellings in quoted material have been silently corrected and punctuation added where necessary.

Jane Kamensky is assistant professor of American history at
Brandeis University. Professor Kamensky has contributed articles to various scholarly journals and anthologies and is the
author of the forthcoming book, *Governing the Tongue: Speech
and Society in Early New England,* which will be published by
Oxford University Press. She earned her B.A. and Ph.D. from
Yale University, where she was an Andrew W. Mellon Foundation Fellow.

Nancy F. Cott is Stanley Woodward Professor of history and
American studies at Yale University. She is the author of *The
Bonds of Womanhood: "Woman's Sphere" in New England
1780–1835, The Grounding of Modern Feminism,* and *A
Woman Making History: Mary Ritter Beard Through Her Let-
ters;* editor of *Root of Bitterness: Documents of the Social His-
tory of American Women;* and co-editor of *A Heritage of Her
Own: Toward a New Social History of American Women.*